Yummy & Easy Diabetes Cookbook and Meal Plans

Diabetic Recipes, Daily Diabetes Menus, Breakfast, Lunch, Dinner & Snacks

Sugar-Free, Glycemic Index-Friendly Blood Sugar Diet

By

Rachael Gordon

Copyright © Ravenna Publishing House, 2021

All Rights Reserved.

Without limiting the rights under the copyright laws, no part of this publication may be reproduced, stored in or introduced into a retrieval system, or transmitted, in any form or by any means (electronic, mechanical, photocopying, recording or otherwise), without the prior written consent of the publisher of this book.

Savona Carrara Publishing House publishes its books and guides in a variety of electronic and print formats, Some content that appears in print may not be available in electronic format, and vice versa.

Designed by Renee Morgan

First Edition

Contents

Dedication and Special Thanks 10

Introduction 12

    Types of Diabetes 15

    Potential Symptoms to Expect 17

    Enjoying a Better Life as a Diabetic Patient 19

    Potential Risks Associated with Being a Diabetic Senior 22

    Enhancing the Recovery Steps 23

The Basics of Diabetes Dieting 26

    Belly Fat – A Major Diabetic Threat 28

    Diabetes Diets 30

        Meals to Embrace 32

        Meals with Healthy Fats 32

        Fiber-Rich Diets 33

        Meals to Avoid 34

        Cholesterol-Rich Meals 34

        Sodium 34

        Saturated Fatty Food 35

        Trans Fats 35

    Understanding the Glycemic Index 35

Opting for Fiber-Packed Meals 39

What to Do if You Have a Sweet Tooth 41

Selecting the Right Fats 45

Building Companionship with Your Food Journal 48

Diabetes Diet Preparation *49*

Steps to Creating/Preparing Your Meal Plan 50

   Step 1 – Identify the Food Required for Each Mealtime 50

   Step 2 – Use the Right Portion Size 53

   Step 3 – Design Your Diabetes Diet Menu 59

Creating a 30-Day Diet Plan *60*

Week 1 Diabetic Meal Plan 62

   Day 1 – Monday 62

   Day 2 – Tuesday 64

   Day 3 – Wednesday 66

   Day 4 – Thursday 68

   Day 5 – Friday 70

   Day 6 – Saturday 72

   Day 7 – Sunday 74

Week 2 Diabetic Meal Plan 76

   Day 8 – Monday 76

   Day 9 – Tuesday 78

   Day 10 – Wednesday 80

Day 11 – Thursday 82

Day 12 – Friday 84

Day 13 – Saturday 86

Day 14 – Sunday 87

Week 3 Diabetic Meal Plan 89

Day 15 – Monday 89

Day 16 – Tuesday 91

Day 17 – Wednesday 93

Day 18 – Thursday 95

Day 19 – Friday 97

Day 20 – Saturday 99

Day 21 – Sunday 101

Week 4 Diabetic Meal Plan 103

Day 22 – Monday 103

Day 23 – Tuesday 105

Day 24 – Wednesday 107

Day 25 – Thursday 109

Day 26 – Friday 111

Day 27 – Saturday 112

Day 28 – Sunday 114

Week 5 Diabetic Meal Plan 116

Day 29 – Monday 116

Day 30 – Tuesday 118

Diabetes Meal Recipes for Breakfast..*121*

   1/2 recipe Blueberry Blast Smoothie 123

   Mixed Berry Salad..124

   Applegurt 126

   Apple Muffins 128

   Strawberry and Tofu Smoothie 131

   Blueberry Compote...133

   Peach French Toast Bake..135

   Healthy Carrot Muffin..137

   Bagel Avocado Toast...140

   Healthy Carrot Muffins 143

   Lemon Bread 146

   Spinach and Egg Scramble with Raspberries......................150

   Baked Banana-Nut Oatmeal..153

   Mediterranean Breakfast Sandwich 157

   Blueberry-Lemon Crumb Muffins.......................................161

Diabetes Meal Recipes for Lunch *166*

   Spring Vegetable and Herbed Chicken Soup 167

   Jicama Salad 170

Mushroom Barley and Roasted Asparagus Salad 172

Escarole and Beans Soup 176

Halibut and Chickpea Salad 177

Lentil and Rice Salad 180

Manhattan Clam Chowder 182

Pumpernickel, Ham, and Watercress Sandwich...................185

Minestrone Soup with Pasta, Beans, and Vegetables 186

Waldorf Salad 189

Raspberry Chicken Salad 192

Chicken Kebabs..194

Chicken (with Tabbouleh) 196

Slow-Roasted Salmon with Cucumber Dill Salad 199

Greek Salad with Oregano Marinated Chicken 202

Open Face Lean Roast Beef Sandwich 207

Spicy Bean Soup...209

Poached Salmon with Lemon Mint Tzatziki 213

Beet and Mandarin Orange Salad with Mint 217

Chicken and Pasta Soup 218

Chickpea and Spinach Salad with Cumin Dressing and Yogurt

Sauce 221

Yogurt with Orange Essence: 224

Diabetes Meal Recipes for Dinner 225

Grilled Ratatouille..228

Grilled Tuna Steaks with Black Sesame Seeds.....................230

Angel Food Cake with Mango Sauce...................................232

Grilled Chicken with Tomato-Cucumber Salad....................234

Baked Mahi Mahi with Wine and Herbs 238

Thai Style Shrimp Stir-Fry with Tomatoes and Basil............240

Garlic-Lime Chicken with Olives 244

Snapper with Roasted Grape Tomatoes, Garlic, and Basil....247

Chopped Nicoise Salad...250

Oven-Baked Parmesan French Fries 254

Pork Au Poivre 257

Ginger Tea Cake 259

Grilled Salad with Herbed Vinaigrette 263

Banana Cream Pie..265

Turkey Burgers with Tomato Corn Salsa 269

Crispy Chicken Fingers 272

Seared Greens with Red Onion and Vinegar 275

Diabetes Meal Recipes for Snacks *277*

Grilled Pita Triangles 280

Chunky Guacamole 281

Hot Chocolate 283

Salsa 285

Blueberry Cake and Banana-Nut Oatmeal Cups 287

Soy-Lime Roasted Tofu 289

Conclusion *291*

Dedication and Special Thanks

This book is dedicated to my late Uncle Phil, who struggled with diabetes for years. I saw the havoc this disease can have on someone's lifestyle and body. It's not easy, but with the proper support system, you can get through anything in life. Uncle Phil taught me that I should pursue life to the fullest. He inspired me to write. He inspired me to cook. I have combined these passions into this book as a labor of love.

I must mention my mother and praise her with special thanks. Without her undying love and support, I quite literally would not be here today. If you have a loving and supporting mother figure in your life, hug her today and tell her how much she means to you.

Finally, I would like to give special thanks to my "Living with Diabetes" Facebook group. These wonderful people have answered countless questions for me about the practicality of living daily with diabetes. Thank you!

Finally, last but not least, I thank you – the reader of this book – for your purchase. Would you do me a small favor? Could you please leave a review online where you made your purchase? Online reviews by verified purchasers help my book reach a wider audience while also providing me with valuable feedback. Thank you in advance!

Introduction

Diabetes is a medical condition that affects your blood sugar levels by creating complications with the hormone insulin. Do you know what makes it worse? It poses additional health problems as you get older. Diabetics of all ages find it difficult to keep track of their diet and blood sugar levels. If you battle this condition, then you have to keep a close watch on your health as you age. It is worth noting that this medical condition affects sight and activities. You may have challenges inspecting product labels, which may require prescription glasses. Exercises may also be difficult to maintain.

Diabetics have almost quadrupled in number since 1980. The disease is spreading around the world, particularly in low- and middle-income countries. There are many causes for this, including a rise in the number of people who are overweight and also overall reduced physical activity. Diabetes, in any manner, can cause complications in a variety of body systems and increase the likelihood of untimely death. In 2012, diabetes was the direct cause of 1.5 million deaths globally.

In April 2016, the World Health Organization (WHO) released a global survey on diabetes, urging action to reduce susceptibility to known risk factors for type 2 diabetes and to improve access to and medical standards for people with diabetes of all types. When handling your insulin, you might still be struggling with new health and mobility concerns. A healthy diet, regular physical activity, maintaining a healthy body weight, and avoiding tobacco use will also help to prevent diabetes and its complications.

Around 422 million people worldwide suffer from

diabetes. In the last three decades, the figure has shown no signs of slowing down. It's worth noting that this medical disorder comes in two types: no insulin development and inadequate insulin use. Type 2 diabetes has its origins in the latter. On the other hand, there is no known cause or identification of risk factors when it comes to type 1 diabetes. Worse, there has been no progress in solving this issue.

As unexpected as it might be, there is a third form of diabetes called gestational diabetes. Hyperglycemia is the cause. Patients with this disorder have an increase in blood sugar content that is smaller than normal diabetes symptoms. During pregnancy and childbirth, pregnant women can encounter complications. There is even a greater probability of having type 2 diabetes in the future.

Here's another fact you should be aware of - the more you go without checking your blood sugar, the more likely you are to experience complications. The key to staying safe at home when you age is to maintain a healthy balance of physical, behavioral, and mental well-being. Here are a few suggestions for integrating healthy living practices into our everyday lives as we age at home.

Types of Diabetes

As discussed before, there are three types of diabetes: type 1 diabetes, type 2 diabetes, and gestational diabetes.

Type 1 diabetes was once known as juvenile-onset diabetes because it most often strikes children, but it can affect anyone at any age. In type 1 diabetes, the human system targets the insulin-producing cells in the pancreas, resulting in a lack of insulin production. Sugar builds up in the body as a result.

Type 2 diabetes seems to be the most frequent. Even though it can occur at any age, it is most common in people over the age of 40. Despite being a milder form of diabetes than type 1, type 2 diabetes will also cause serious health problems. Overweight people are at the greatest risk of having type 2 diabetes. Diabetes has no known treatment. Type 2 diabetes, on the other hand, can be regulated and treated by diet, nutrition, and exercise. If not managed well, type 2 diabetes will worsen, and medications are often needed. Further medical complications can still occur, even with medication.

Gestational diabetes is caused by hormonal fluctuations during pregnancy. Although we don't know what causes gestational diabetes, we do know that it occurs when the body is unable to produce and use the insulin required for pregnancy, resulting in elevated blood sugar levels. But don't be alarmed. Individuals with diabetes will live a regular, stable life if they notice the medical condition early and keep it under control. There are cost-effective treatment conditions available to support certain individuals in diagnosing and treating this disease through a range of treatments, including:

Harm to the skin, feet, and kidneys should be examined daily.

Controlling blood glucose levels by a combination of food, physical exercise, and, in rare situations, medicine. An A1C test compares the blood glucose levels over the last three months. The A1C test can help diagnose diabetes as well as track and control levels of people who already have it. The examination, which can be performed daily in conjunction with a diagnosis, would also determine when your prescriptions need to be changed.

Controlling blood pressure and lipids helps to lower the risk of coronary disease and other complications.

An A1C test compares the blood glucose levels over the last three months. The A1C test can help diagnose diabetes as well as track and control levels of people who already have it. The examination, which can be performed daily in conjunction with a diagnosis, would also determine when your prescriptions need to be changed.

Potential Symptoms to Expect

Diabetes signs stem from high blood sugar levels. Common symptoms include:

Heightened hunger

Increased thirst and hazy vision

Urination regularly

Tiredness

Unexplained weight loss

Skin infections or late healing sores

Hand and foot tingling or numbness

When your blood sugar levels are too high, you run the risk of destroying your organs and tissues all. Inactivity with regard to weight, family medical history, high blood pressure, and many more are risk factors. The higher your blood sugar level is and the longer you go without treatment, the most likely you are to develop problems such as:

Stroke

Dementia

Depression

Vision Loss

Hearing loss

Skin Conditions

Heart Attack/Heart Disease

Enjoying a Better Life as a Diabetic Patient

Diabetes is a progressive condition with no cure. However, it is not a crippling disease. Even at an old age, you can control this medical condition to sustain a healthier lifestyle. You may not 'personally' detect diabetes or prediabetes until it becomes full-blown. For this reason, it is essential to undergo medical examinations regularly. Take a blood sugar test consistently to keep an eye on your system. Monitoring and managing blood sugar in older adults is more effectively accomplished through diet and exercise.

Fortunately, you can follow the precautions at home without the need for a prescription or pricey supplies. These habits not only help you maintain a stable blood glucose level, but they also help you avoid other problems. You might also benefit from befriending other elderly individuals who are making similar improvements, in addition to eating healthy and becoming more active. Having a support system with friends will help you stick to your diabetes treatment plan.

But how serious is this medical condition? Here is a shocker. One-quarter of Americans over 65 have diabetes. The other half battle prediabetes. Expect this figure to skyrocket in the coming decades as the number of confirmed patients hits 23.1 million. Surprisingly, about 7.2 million undiagnosed cases are prevalent in the United States alone. Where does this leave us? About 23.8 percent of diabetics are, in truth, unaware of their condition. That is a staggering amount.

Several approaches exist in addressing diabetes. The first step involves consuming healthy meals. Another option is to undergo medication. Some individuals combine both food and medication to improve their well-being. By keeping track of your A1C, you can determine when to adjust your drugs or meals. A glucometer will help you monitor your body's insulin needs, calculate your glucose levels, and discuss your optimal recovery strategy with your doctor. Contact the physician immediately if there are any changes in your skin or well-being. You may also visit a nutritionist, optometry expert (vision), endocrinologists (endocrine system), and podiatrists, alongside other health practitioners, to explore the diabetes treatment strategies.

Maintaining a healthy lifestyle is one of the easiest ways to reduce diabetes complications. So, be sure your fitness, food, and self-monitoring are high on the regular priority list if you're a senior with diabetes. Don't forget to exercise regularly. It is a fantastic way to naturally balance your blood sugar. At the same time, you don't have to undertake a difficult exercise. Taking a short walk after each meal can go a long way to help regulate your blood sugar level. Remember that basic carbohydrates and sugars are a no-no. Avoid these substances if you want to improve your overall well-being. Cut back on starch intake as well. Focus mainly on vegetables, protein, dairy, and other products that may worsen your condition.

Remember that other parts of your body count. As a diabetic patient, you may also have problems with your skin, feet, and mouth. Ensure to conduct medical examinations regularly. Don't miss your appointments.

Potential Risks Associated with Being a Diabetic Senior

Do you know that diabetics in their forties, fifties, and older are more likely than their younger counterparts to die early? That's not all. They have a higher risk of losing their physical capacity or muscle mass than elderly non-diabetics. Such individuals have a higher risk of having coexisting illnesses, like coronary heart disease or asthma, as well as end-stage renal failure. Older diabetics are more likely to collapse or experience a stroke, as well as suffer from urinary incontinence, cognitive impairment, chronic pain, and polypharmacy (multiple medications for the same condition.) Any of these medical conditions may affect their ability to control diabetes and overall health.

Diabetes increases the risk of cognitive decline in seniors, which can range from minor executive dysfunction to dementia. According to researchers, poor glycemic control is linked to deteriorating cognitive function. What does this mean? The longer you live with this medical condition, the more likely your cognitive function will deteriorate. It is still unknown how diabetes onset later in life affects cognitive function. Self-care, on the other hand, becomes a major concern for diabetics as their condition worsens. You may have a problem regulating blood sugar levels, adjusting insulin doses, and maintaining a healthy diet.

Enhancing the Recovery Steps

If you have a long list of challenges affecting your fitness and ability to care for your future self, all you need is a personalized plan. Ideally, elderly diabetics should be screened for diabetes complications, according to physicians. It is a smart idea to get tested for depression and geriatric syndromes like cognitive dysfunction. If you use insulin, you understand how important it is to have strong perceptual, sensory, and motor skills.

Essentially, you have to harness them to achieve their specific glycemic goals with the help of your doctor. By doing so, it reduces hypoglycemia, a significant risk that diabetes experts are now researching. Multiple daily injections can become too problematic at any stage if you have advanced diabetes complications, decreased working capability, or other issues. Find out from your doctor if once-daily basal insulin doses are effective to prevent the downsides associated with too many injection jabs.

What is a good recovery process without diet and nutrition? There is not enough content that can cover the entirety of this subject or iterate its importance. Diabetes patients have the same dietary requirements as everybody else. To keep your diabetes under check, make sure your meals are well cooked. Fruits, vegetables, lean meats, and whole grains can all be consumed in reasonable quantities. Type 1 diabetes and younger-onset Type 2 diabetics will need to tweak their nutrition regimens to maintain their bodies' shifting needs. It includes avoiding desserts and sugary beverages, nonetheless preparing meals from scratch. The timing of your insulin dosage can be dictated by your diet and exercise. However, it also centers around your level of diabetes. To preserve optimal blood sugar/insulin balance, Doctors typically recommend three small meals with snacks in between.

Do you know that exercising daily under medical supervision reduces the risk of co-existing health problems? Underlying medical conditions may make diabetes management more complex. To avoid complications, you should get your muscles and bones in optimum form and functionality through light exercises. If you're out of shape or have health issues, your blood pressure will eventually stabilize if you get moving regularly. Start small and work up to 10 to 15 minutes of physical activity a day. Go on a hike, a swim, or a bike ride. Increase your time when you do these regularly.

> Your social life also counts. Social isolation of any kind may have a significant impact on your freedom and quality of life. Hence, you should create a strong social support network and include them in joint decision-making. Your way of life affects diabetes treatment and care. If you are an older diabetic adult or have been diagnosed with diabetes for a long time, controlling the disease takes careful preparation. Managing diabetes entails more than merely maintaining a healthy blood sugar level. Over time, the disorder can become more difficult to treat. However, if you start early and stick to it, you can prevent a lot of issues later in the future. This book takes care of the first recovery process – diet, meal preparations, and recipes.

The Basics of Diabetes Dieting

Now that you understand what there is to know about diabetes and how to manage it, it's time to talk about diabetes diets. To start, what exactly is a diabetes diet? Diabetes dieting distinctly entails consuming the healthiest meals in moderation and adhering to a daily meal schedule. A diabetic diet is a nutritious, low-fat, low-calorie diet plan that is naturally high in nutrients. Fruits, herbs, and whole grains are essential components.

A diabetes diet is, in reality, the safest dietary strategy for nearly all individuals.

You don't need any special diets if you're trying to avoid or regulate diabetes. It is more prevalent if your dietary requirements are generalized; in other words, the same as everyone else. But even at that, you have to closely monitor your food choices, including the carbohydrates you consume. Even though most dieticians recommend adopting a Meditteranean or other heart-healthy diets, you also have to incorporate a weight-loss program that addresses potential factors, like obesity and overweight. Why is this important? You may question. Here is a fact: dropping only 5 percent to 10 percent of your total weight will lower your blood sugar, blood pressure, and cholesterol levels.

Losing weight and eating a healthier diet can improve your morale, stamina, and a general sense of well-being. Diabetes patients have an almost doubled risk of heart disease. But that is not all. They are more likely to suffer mental health conditions, such as depression. In a vast number of cases, type 2 diabetes can be prevented, and in some cases, it can also be reversed. So, it's not too late if you've already been diagnosed with diabetes. You can choose to live healthily. To do that, you need to eat well, become more physically active, and gain weight (muscle). These steps alleviate the effects of diabetes.

Does that imply that you should starve or skip meals? Definitely, not. You don't have to (and should not) engage in unhealthy practices to control diabetes and its symptoms. Diabetes dieting entails enjoying a sumptuous, well-balanced diet that provides you with more energy and improves your mental state. You don't have to settle for boring meals or put your candies in the trash bin. Speaking of meals, your diet should contain significant amounts of nutrients. Each food we consume is packed with nutrients and calories. They may either have positive or negative effects on the body. Overweight, kidney defects, respiratory dysfunction, stroke, heart disease, vision deficiency, and nerve damage or disability stem mostly from the constant intake of calorie-dense diets.

Belly Fat – A Major Diabetic Threat

Belly fat is a health problem that affects millions of

people around the world. The majority of people try unsuccessfully to get rid of it. It can be humiliating to get belly fat. That, though, is just the tip of the iceberg. This health problem not only affects a person's look but also poses several health hazards. Being overweight or obese is the most significant risk factor for type 2 diabetes. You are at greater risk if you choose to bear your weight around your stomach rather than your shoulders and thighs. One of the things that make belly fat dangerous is that it settles around the stomach organs and liver, which is linked to insulin resistance. Once there is no insulin production or utilization, you stand a risk of having diabetes. You can tell that you are at the borderline of this medical condition,

If, as a man, you have a waist circumference of at least 40 inches.

If, as a woman, you have a 35-inch waist circumference or more.

Do you also know that fructose calories (found in sugary beverages including soda, energy, and sports drinks, coffee drinks, and refined foods like doughnuts, muffins, cookies, fruit, and granola bars) are more prone to trigger belly fat development? Presumably, you never imagined that your favorite cookie brand came with a "disclaimer," one not printed on the pack. Having a sweet tooth comes with several challenges, including avoiding sugar-rich products. Nevertheless, cutting down on sugary foods will help you lose weight and reduce the risk of diabetes.

Diabetes Diets

A diabetic diet consists of three meals per day, consumed at regular intervals. This helps to make better use of the insulin your body generates or receives from a prescription. Certified dietitians assist diabetic patients in developing diets that are tailored to their fitness needs, preferences, and lifestyles. They may also give expert counsel on ways to change dietary habits, such as selecting portion sizes that are appropriate for one's height and level of exercise. One problem diabetics face is the inability to maintain a healthy lifestyle. It stems from a far-fetched belief that managing diabetes means giving up everything and sticking to a miserly life. You have to know where to draw the thin line.

For example, most people believe that diabetes patients must avoid sugar at all times. But here is the truth: you can enjoy any snack of choice, provided that you make preparations ahead and reduce hidden sugars. In truth, your favorite desserts could be a part of your regular diet. You don't have to slam the "Nope" button every time, except you have a problem monitoring and managing your intake. Another misconception is that people assume that diabetic patients automatically eliminate carb consumption overnight in a bid to manage their conditions.

The sort of carbohydrates you eat, as well as the volume of food you consume, are important. So why dump a meal when you can change specific aspects of it. Instead of starchy carbohydrates, use whole-grain carbohydrates, which are high in fiber and digest slowly, resulting in more stable blood sugar levels.

Your meals do not have to be expensive to create a diabetic dietary plan. There are no seeming added benefits in first-class diabetic diets. Meals from both ends of the financial spectrum provide the same result, depending on how you combine and take them. And if someone out there tells you that maintaining a strict diabetes diet involves consuming protein-rich diets solely, kindly double-check on that. Research has shown that consuming too much protein, especially animal protein, can lead to insulin resistance, which is a key factor in diabetes. Protein, carbs, and fats are also essential components in a good diet. To work properly, our bodies need all three. The secret is to eat a well-balanced diet.

Meals to Embrace

Health meal intake helps you to make the most of your calories. Balanced carbs, fiber-rich meats, seafood, and "healthy" fats are good choices.

Meals with Healthy Fats

Are you looking to lower your cholesterol? Monounsaturated and polyunsaturated fats should be emphasized in your diet. Nuts, avocados, peanut, olive, and canola oils are some of the ingredients in these dishes. To avoid excessive calorie buildup, though, keep the intake to a minimum.

Fiber-Rich Diets

All portions of plant foods that your body cannot absorb or digest are considered dietary fibers. Fiber helps regulate blood sugar levels by controlling how the body digests. Meals in this category include:

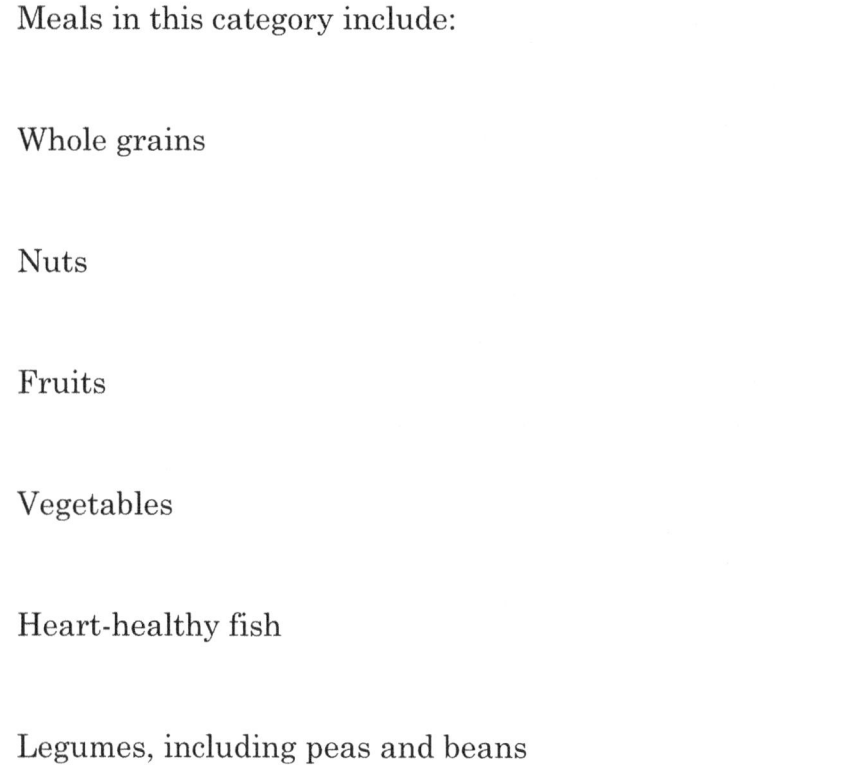

Whole grains

Nuts

Fruits

Vegetables

Heart-healthy fish

Legumes, including peas and beans

Not all fish count. Some of them have high-mercury content, an example being the king mackerel. However, others are healthy for the heart. They prevent the risk of heart disease, thanks to the presence of omega-3 fatty acids. Such fish include mackerel, sardines, salmon, and tuna.

Meals to Avoid

Your meals affect your system indirectly. In what way? You may ask. Here is one angle you may skip, unintentionally. Diabetes accelerates the formation of clogged and hardened arteries, increasing the risk of heart attack and stroke. Foods containing the ingredients listed below will help you reach your goal of eating a heart-healthy diet.

Cholesterol-Rich Meals

Cholesterol levels are elevated in non-fat dairy and animal fats, egg yolks, kidneys, and other organ meats. Limit your cholesterol intake to no more than 200 milligrams per day (mg).

Sodium

Sodium is a mineral found in many foods. One of the ways you can treat diabetes is to monitor your sodium intake. Ideally, it should be less than 2,300 mg. If you have high blood pressure, your doctor can advise you to reach for even less.

Saturated Fatty Food

High-fat dairy ingredients, as well as animal proteins like steak, sausage, hot dogs, butter, and bacon, should be off your list. You may also want to cut back on your palm kernel and coconut oil intake.

Trans Fats

Trans fats exist in baked goods, packaged snacks, and shortening and stick margarine. They are unhealthy. As such, you should avoid them.

Understanding the Glycemic Index

Have you heard of the term "Glycemic Index?" If yes, how can you interpret it? Think of the glycemic index being a scale – a measuring system. What is its function? GI evaluates and measures in order the carbohydrate quantity in foods. This rating goes from zero to 100. You can use this metric system to determine what meals are prone to increasing blood sugar. Meals at the higher end of the spectrum raise blood sugar quickly and vice-versa. Even though this rating system has long been touted as a way to regulate blood sugar effectively, it has several downsides.

The GI's real health effects are still uncertain.

Eating becomes overly difficult when you have to consult GI tables.

There is a thin line that defines the confines of GI as a metric system. Unfortunately, it provides a direct evaluation of the safety of a meal.

The GI isn't a metric on how safe a meal is. According to the study, merely adopting the Mediterranean or other heart-healthy diet recommendations will help you lower your glycemic load while still enhancing the consistency of your diet.

What foods have a low glycemic index?

Bulgar

Barley

Muesli

Lentils

Legumes

Oat Bran

Most fruit

Steel-cut oatmeal

Brown or wild rice

Whole-grain pasta

Lima beans or butter beans

Non-starchy veggies, including carrots and sweet potatoes

Whole grains, including pita bread, pumpernickel bread,

and whole-wheat bread.

Meals with high GI include the following:

Puffed rice

Instant oatmeal

Popcorn

Pumpkin

Pretzels

Saltine crackers

Corn flakes

Pineapple

Melons

Bran flakes

Starchy veggies, such as potatoes.

Heavily-processed grains, including white pasta, white bread, and white rice.

A low GI diet will help those with diabetes, those seeking to lose weight, and those at risk of heart disease. The effects are also advantageous to all, not just individuals with chronic illnesses. The GI will assist a person in making healthy dietary and nutritional choices. A low-GI diet does not necessitate the exclusion of all high-GI ingredients. Instead, a person's target should be to maintain consistency over time, with a heavy emphasis on high-fiber, low-GI foods. A doctor or dietitian will assist you in creating a tasty and nourishing diet that includes a range of low-GI foods.

Opting for Fiber-Packed Meals

Don't you think that it is high time you stored away those unhealthy food products? Are there alternatives in their place? Of course, yes. You have several healthy options, some of which are listed below.

Spaghetti squash or whole-wheat pasta are great replacements for regular pasta.

Consume low-sugar bran flakes in place of cornflakes.

Why stick to your white bread when you can enjoy whole-grain or whole-wheat bread?

Riced cauliflower, brown rice, or wild rice can replace white rice.

Grab your leafy greens or peas and discard those corn cobs.

Enjoy your breakfast with a bowl of high-fiber, low-sugar cereal instead of sugary cereal.

Cauliflower mash, yams, and sweet potatoes can take the place of French fries and mashed white potatoes.

How about replacing instant oatmeal with rolled or steel-cut oats? That sounds great, right?

What to Do if You Have a Sweet Tooth

It is easy to read instructions from a book on stopping this and avoiding that. The main challenge comes when you attempt to adhere to those guidelines. Of course, you cannot give up your M&M's or Skittles in one night just because some dieticians said so. The struggle is real when it boils down to taking action. However, you need the right approach to deal with your cravings. As stated before, just because you want to stick to a diabetic diet plan does not mean that you should flush your "favorites" down the drain.

Often, the problem with sugar consumption is that it is in excess – more than required. You can cut back on your sugar meal servings. Why have three cans of soda a day when you can enjoy one per week to maintain good health? Gradually reduce the sugar content in your diet, one calorie at a time. By doing so, your taste buds can adjust to your new meals effectively. If you want cake, put the bread (or rice or pasta) on hold. Sweets add additional carbs to a meal, so limit other carb-heavy meals at the same time. You can include healthy fats, as they delay metabolism. Your blood sugar levels don't rise quickly. As interesting as this sounds, you don't necessarily have to go for the cake. Enjoy other options, like yogurt, peanut butter, almonds, and ricotta cheese.

Instead of snacking on candy alone, eat them with a meal. Sweets induce an increase in blood sugar when taken on their own. On the other hand, blood sugar would not increase quickly if you consume them alongside other nutritious foods at the same time. When last did you indulge your mind into your meals? Do you consume breakfast, lunch, and dinner absent-mindedly?

Such acts can lead to overeating, affecting your weight and other health aspects. So, this is what to do to counter such an unhealthy habit. Put your mind into whatever you eat, savoring your meal with each bite. Do you have a huge slice of cake on your plate? Enjoy its taste and texture. Don't be in a hurry. By doing this, you can enjoy your meal without going overboard with your stomach.

There is that one drink that some of us cannot seem to get our hands off, even if it means struggling with that health condition. It's challenging – no doubt. But there is always a way around such problems. Reduce the intake of soft drinks, sweet foods, and juice. Each 12 oz. serving of sugar-sweetened soda you consume every day increases the risk of diabetes by around 15%. Try sparkling water with a squeeze of lemon or lime instead. Reduce how much creamer and sweetener you place in your tea and coffee. Avoid substituting processed carbohydrates for saturated fat, such as whole milk dairy. It is not a better option.

Sugar is not an ideal replacement for saturated fat. Create your 'own' sugar replacements. Purchase unflavored oatmeal, plain yogurt, or unsweetened ice tea and sweeten to taste, using sweeteners or fruits. You will also need less sugar than the recipe calls for, regardless of the meal type.

Inspect the packaging of any food product you intend to purchase. Use low-sugar options instead of packaged foods. Pay close attention to the sugar level of your cereals and sugary beverages. Steer clear of boxed or processed items that may contain added sugar. Those frozen meals, canned soups, or low-fat food with hidden sugar should be off your dieting list. Homemade meals are ideal replacements. Curtail the sugar content in recipes. Use other sugar replacements, like vanilla extract, nutmeg, mint, and cinnamon. Getting rid of your sweet tooth is not a walk in the park. It is not an overnight event. You do not wake up one morning to discover that you no longer crave sweets, cakes, and sodas.

To feed your sweet tooth, look for healthier alternatives. Blend frozen bananas to make a smooth, frozen dessert instead of ice cream. Alternatively, instead of a milk chocolate chip, nibble on a little piece of dark chocolate. Begin with half of your usual dessert and cover the other portion with fruit. Being aware of the dangers of sugar is just a journey half completed.

There are other factors to note. Sugar is also present in a variety of fast food meals, packaged foods, and supermart necessities. Such products can include baked goods, cereals, pizza, ketchup, low-fat meals, frozen dinner, oven-mashed potatoes, and margarine. Your first stop should be on the food labels. Look for hidden sugar content; this can be daunting, but it is worth the task.

But why is there hidden sugar and displayed sugar

content? You may wonder. Manufacturers are required to display the total sugar amount on their packaging. However, they are not mandated to differentiate between added sugar and sugar found naturally in the product. There is a subtle display of added sugars on the pack. How can you tell the ingredients that belong to this group?

When you lift your food product, do you see items like syrup, invert sugar, cane crystals, evaporated cane juice, lactose, dextrose, fructose, maltose, corn sweetener, and agave nectar? These items are classified as added sugars. While you would expect sugar to be placed at the top of the product list, manufacturers use various types of added sugars that are then scattered across the list. What is the result? Both of these small doses of various sweeteners will add extra sugar and empty calories.

Selecting the Right Fats

Often, "fats" have a negative connotation. However, not all fats are unhealthy. There are healthy fats as well. These substances are present in our food. Unhealthy fats, also known as saturated fats, are present in red meat, dairy, and tropical oils. Your meals may not be 'free from saturated fats. You don't have to be worried about that. Ensure that you enjoy your meals in moderation. According to the American Diabetes Association, your calorie intake from saturated fat should not exceed 10 percent per day.

Healthy or unsaturated fats are present in plants and fish. Some sources include nuts, olive oil, and avocados. Omega-3 fatty acids are anti-inflammatory and helpful to the brain and heart. You can get this substance from tuna, flaxseeds, and salmon.

Here are some ways to get rid of unhealthy fats:

Avoid frying your food to prevent cholesterol buildup. Stir-fry, bake, or broil it.

Enjoy delicious treats like seeds or nuts, including nut butter. You can add them to your breakfast cereal.

Your salads and sandwiches should contain avocados. You may also prepare guacamole, a satisfying that contains healthy fats.

Replace red meat with eggs, skinless chicken, protein-sourced veggies, and eggs.

Consume dairy moderately.

Try homemade salad dressings, pasta dishes, or cooked veggies containing sesame, flaxseed, or olive oil.

Do you want tremendous results? Maintain a diet log and eat daily. It is reassuring to hear that losing only 7 percent of your body weight will cut your risk of diabetes in half. You do not have to obsessively count calories or go on a diet to do this. Following a regular eating schedule and keeping track of what you eat are two of the most effective strategies. When you follow a daily meal schedule, the body controls weight gain or loss and blood sugar levels.

For each meal, aim for a portion size that is small and constant. Each day should start with a savoring, healthy meal to get energy and stabilize blood sugar levels. Maintain the same calorie consumption. Rather than overeating every day or at one meal and then missing the next, try to eat about the same amount every day and keep blood sugar levels in order.

Building Companionship with Your Food Journal

Having a food diary is essential to maintaining a healthy diet. According to a recent survey, people who kept a diet diary lost weight twice as much as someone who did not. Why is that? A written log will help you find places where you're eating more calories than you know, such as your midday snack or morning latte. It also makes you more mindful of what, why, and how much you are eating, which will help you stop mindless snacking. You can monitor your diet via your food journal or an app.

While you keep track of your diet, ensure that you exercise regularly. This activity gives you more control over your weight and enhances insulin sensitivity. To start your workout journey, walk 30 minutes or 10 minutes (three times) each day. Try out cycling, swimming, or any other simple activity.

Diabetes Diet Preparation

We discussed diabetes dieting in the first chapter, including meals, glycemic index (GI), belly fat, and ways to manage your sweet tooth. Before then, we had covered everything you need to know about diabetes, including description, types, and causes. Even though we discussed some meals in those previous chapters, you need to know an ideal diet plan to get started. This section teaches you how to create a customized meal plan. Perhaps, you have something else in mind to prepare and aren't sure how to organize your meals, here's what you can do.

Steps to Creating/Preparing Your Meal Plan

Step 1 – Identify the Food Required for Each Mealtime

Each mealtime comes with its unique food, which may comprise fruits, protein, leafy greens, vegetables, protein snacks, starch or grain, and taste enhancers. These small food components determine each meal structure, making it easy to know what to eat per time. It is also worth noting that each food has its calorie level.

Diet Plan Containing 1200 Calories

Breakfast – includes 1 protein, 1 fruit, and vegetables (optional).

Lunch – includes 1 protein, 1 leafy green, 1 vegetable, and 1 taste enhancer.

Snack – includes 1 protein snack and 1 fruit or vegetable.

Dinner – includes 1 protein, 1 leafy green, 1 starch/grain,

1 taste enhancer, and 2 vegetables.

Snack – includes 1 fruit.

Diet Plan Containing 1500 Calories

Breakfast – includes 1 protein, 1 fruit, and vegetables (optional).

Lunch – includes 1 protein, leafy greens, 1 starch, 1 vegetable, 1 fruit, and 1 taste enhancer.

Snack – includes 1 protein snack and 1 vegetable.

Dinner – includes 1 starch/grain, leafy greens, 2 protein, 2 vegetables, and 1 taste enhancer.

Snack – includes 1 fruit.

Diet Plan Containing 1800 Calories

Breakfast – includes 1 protein, 1 fruit, and vegetables (optional).

Snack – includes 1 protein snack.

Lunch – includes 1 starch/grain, leafy greens, 2 protein, 2 vegetables, 1 fruit, and 1 taste enhancer.

Snack – 1 protein snack and 1 fruit or vegetable.

Dinner – 1 starch/grain, leafy greens, 2 vegetables, 2 protein, and 1 taste enhancer.

Snack – 1 fruit.

Diet Plan Containing 2200 Calories

Breakfast – includes 2 proteins, 1 starch/grain, 1 fruit, and vegetables (optional).

Snack – includes 1 protein snack.

Lunch – includes 2 vegetables, 2 proteins, 1 starch/grain, 1 fruit, leafy greens, and 1 taste enhancer.

Snack – includes 1 protein snack and 1 fruit or vegetable.

Dinner – includes 2 proteins, 2 vegetables, 2 starch/grain, leafy greens, and 2 taste enhancers.

Snack – includes 1 fruit.

Step 2 – Use the Right Portion Size

The next step is to familiarize yourself with the serving sizes within and of the food groups until you have worked out the simple rundown of your meal plan. This is one of the most crucial aspects of controlling your calorie intake. Kindly note that each of the following elements counts as one portion in each of the groups.

<u>Fruit</u>

When selecting the type of fruit to use, fresh or frozen fruits come to mind. They provide you with the ideal portion size based on your calorie intake.

1 typical piece of fruit (apple, orange, banana, etc.)

1 dried fruit (small handful)

1 cup (80g) of cut fruit or berries

½ cup (125 ml) 100% fruit juice

Starch or Grain

Except for starchy vegetables (such as corn and peas, which are classified as starches), vegetables have the fewest calories per bite of any product. In truth, the calories in leafy

The foods listed in this group are whole grains. They provide more vitamins, minerals, and fiber than refined "white" starches, like white rice or white bread. Try to choose whole grains whenever possible.

1 whole-grain bread slice

½ potato, white or sweet

1 cup cooked rolled oats (250g)

2 corn tortillas

½ cup (150g) cooked grain (rice, pasta, quinoa, etc.), beans, lentils, corn kernels, or peas

Vegetable

Except for starchy vegetables (such as corn and peas, which are classified as starches), vegetables have the fewest calories per bite of any product. In truth, the calories in leafy greens like lettuce are so low that they can be consumed in any volume.

1 cup (80g) any vegetable

Leafy greens – any amount

Protein

The low-fat proteins listed below are the ones you can eat the most. For example, higher-fat animal products and dairy products would contain more calories.

3 oz. (85g) lean meat or cooked poultry

5 oz. tofu (125 g)

A quarter-pound (4 oz.) (100g) shellfish or fried fish

1 cup (250g) non-fat yogurt (plain or vanilla) or non-fat cottage cheese

1 whole egg, or 4 egg whites

2 scoops Herbalife Formula 1, 1 cup (250 ml) nonfat or low-fat milk

Protein Snacks

Protein snacks have a lower calorie and protein content than a regular protein serving. These smaller protein sources offer "boosts" during the day, which prevents hunger.

1 ounce (30g) roasted soy nuts

1 ounce (30g) low-fat mozzarella cheese

1 Herbalife Protein Snack Bar Deluxe

1 cup (250 ml) nonfat or low-fat milk

½ cup (85 g) edamame soybeans

4 tbsp (60g) hummus

½ cup (125g) non-fat cottage cheese or flavored yogurt

Taste Enhancers

To add spice to your meals, use tiny quantities of fats or sweets. Any of the following foods has 60-75 calories, which is why I keep them to a minimum in my diet plans. While avocado is, in truth, a fruit, it is listed as a flavor enhancer because the majority of its calories come from fat. Similarly, while nuts contain some protein, the bulk of their calories come from fat, so they're listed here.

¼ medium avocado

2 tbsp (30g) ketchup

A small handful of nuts

2 tbsp (30g) light cream for coffee

½ ounce (15g) grated Parmesan cheese

2 tbsp (30g) reduced-calorie salad dressing

1 tbsp (20g) jam, jelly, honey, syrup, and sugar

2 tsp (10 ml) olive, canola, sunflower, or safflower oil

2 tbsp (30g) low-fat sour cream or low-fat mayonnaise

Some foods are called "free" since they have too few calories. Some foods are called "free" since they have too few calories. They include vinegar, mustard, herbs and spices, onion, garlic, lime and lemon juices, soy sauce, Worcestershire sauce, hot pepper sauces, broth or bouillon, horseradish, peppermint and vanilla extracts, calorie-free sweeteners and beverages, and salsa.

Step 3 – Design Your Diabetes Diet Menu

It's time to bring the menu plans together so that you can be comfortable with the serving sizes for the various food categories. You can now add foods from any of the food groups to build your personalized diet plan using the basic framework for the calorie level you choose.

Creating a 30-Day Diet Plan

In this section, there is a 30-day diet plan you can use or customize to commence your real journey to recovery if you don't want to create a custom dietary plan, as discussed in the previous section. Kindly note that the meals for each day fall into three main categories – breakfast, lunch, and dinner. You will also find these meals in their respective various weeks, ranging from one to four. The meal plan in this section will provide you with three meals daily, including snacks. However, understand that your dietary choice may differ from that of another person. When selecting a preference, several factors come into play, including:

You can monitor the progression of diabetes and its symptoms by keeping track of your weight.

Dietary fiber will help you regulate your blood sugar levels and reduce your risk of elevated cholesterol, weight gain, cardiovascular disease, and other health issues.

Manage carbohydrate consumption by maintaining activity levels while using insulin as well as other medicines.

Reduce the consumption of processed carbs and sugar-rich foods, including cookies, sodas, and candies. These products tend to trigger a sugar spike compared to vegetables and whole grains.

Understand the effect of dietary choices on diabetic complications. For example, salt is a trigger of high blood pressure.

Week 1 Diabetic Meal Plan

Day 1 – Monday

Having more soy foods in your diet, such as edamame, can help lower cholesterol. High cholesterol is linked to heart disease, which is a risk factor for diabetics.

Breakfast

1 slice (1 oz.) cooked Canadian bacon

½ cup of sliced mangoes

1 toasted slice of whole wheat raisin bread with ¼ cup part-skim ricotta cheese

Lunch

1 small whole-wheat pita bread

3 oz. sliced turkey

10 red grapes

Mushroom barley and roasted asparagus salad

Dinner

1 small whole-wheat pita bread

3 oz. baked cod

½ cup cooked whole-wheat couscous

Grilled ratatouille (serves 1)

½ cup cooked edamame

1 cup fat-free milk

½ cup sugar-free, low-fat frozen yogurt

1 cup raw spinach with 2 tsp of champagne vinegar and 2 tsp of olive oil.

Day 2 – Tuesday

Fiber is critical for maintaining blood sugar control. High-fiber meals, such as whole-grain pancakes, whole-grain rolls, and brown rice, can help you have a happy and healthy day because fluctuating blood sugar levels will trigger symptoms of hunger, irritability, and low energy.

Breakfast

½ cup of blended berries

2 tsp of sugar-free maple syrup

1 cup of fat-free milk

2 (four-inch) whole grain pancakes

Lunch

1 cup tossed salad and 2 tbsp of low-fat dressing

Spring Vegetable and Herbed Chicken Soup

1 small apple

1 whole-grain roll (1 oz.)

Dinner

½ cup of cubed cucumber and ½ cup of cubed tomato mixtures, flavored with 1 tsp of balsamic vinegar and 2 tsp of olive oil

½ cup of brown rice cooked in low-fat chicken broth

Grilled salmon (4 oz.)

1 (1 oz.) slice rye bread

5 roasted asparagus spears

Snacks

½ cup of melon cubes combined with 1 tsp of lime juice

10 almonds

Day 3 – Wednesday

Breakfast and lunch are crucial. But who says desserts cannot be eaten at dinner? With the help of a dietician, you can have your cake and eat it too. Make dessert a part of your meal schedule.

Breakfast

½ cup cubes blended pineapple, kiwi, and papaya

1 cup nonfat milk

1 whole-wheat pita bread, toasted

2 tsp of jam (sugar-free)

Lunch

Escarole and Bean soup

1 cup tossed salad with 2 tsp mild dressing

½ cup applesauce (no added sugar) coated with cinnamon

1 multigrain bread slice

Dinner

3 oz. of boneless pork loin chop, grilled

½ cup of broccolini sautéed in 1 tsp extra virgin olive oil

Mango cake (Angel Food Cake)

½ cup roasted potatoes (leave the skins on for more fiber!)

Snacks

1 oz. of pretzels (whole wheat)

1 egg (hard-boiled)

You can enjoy delectable, nourishing desserts like Angel Food Cake. To get a boost of vitamin C, serve the meal with some mangoes.

Day 4 – Thursday

Instead of butter or the traditional margarine, use non-hydrogenated spreads like canola margarine on your potatoes, bread, and other foods. Canola margarine has no trans fats, which are a risk factor for heart disease in people with diabetes.

Breakfast

1 oz. of ready-of-eat whole-grain cereal

½ cup of fat-free milk

½ grapefruit broiled

Lunch

1 small peach

Jicama salad (serves 1)

2 oz. low-fat cheddar cheese melted on a whole-wheat

English muffin with 2 tomato slices.

Dinner

3 ounces lean grilled flank steak

½ cup steamed spinach

½ cup baked sweet potato with 1 tsp of canola oil margarine

1 cup romaine lettuce tossed with onions, red peppers, and 2 tbsp of low-calorie dressing

½ baked pear (halve and core an unpeeled pear, put cut-side down in the baking dish, pour low-calorie cranberry juice halfway up the sides, and bake for 30 to 40 minutes at 375 degrees)

Snacks

1 cup low-fat, sugar-free yogurt

2 tsp of reduced-fat peanut butter on 1 oz. whole-grain crackers

Day 5 – Friday

When preparing your meals, don't forget to add vegetables. It's preferable if the hue is darker. The dark leaves of arugula, for example, are high in antioxidants such as beta carotene and vitamin C. These antioxidants protect the heart and are good for diabetics.

Breakfast

2 tsp of reduced-fat cream cheese

1 small (2 oz.) toasted whole wheat bagel

½ cup sugar-free, fat-free yogurt

½ cup sliced fresh strawberries

2 slices tomato

Lunch

1 small peach

½ cup red and yellow bell pepper strips

3 oz. lean roast beef, 1 lettuce leaf, ¼ cup sliced carrots, and 1 tsp of fat-free Ranch or Thousand Island dressing wrapped in a 10-inch whole wheat tortilla.

Dinner

½ cup cooked zucchini and yellow squash sautéed in 1 tsp of olive oil and sprinkled with ¼ tsp of dried oregano

½ cup cooked whole-wheat couscous

1 small orange, sliced

Snacks

1 (½ cup) serving non-sugar vanilla pudding

2 cups of air-popped popcorn

Day 6 – Saturday

Spice up your diet with tuna today. Tuna has a meaty feel and steak-like flavor, making such red meat a great substitute. Tunas are rich in omega-3 fatty acids used to reduce elevated blood cholesterol, an identifiable diabetes risk factor.

Breakfast

½ cup of blueberries sprinkled with ½ tsp of lemon zest

1 cup of fat-free milk

1 tsp of canola oil margarine

1 small bran muffin

Lunch

1 cup of tossed salad with 2 tbsp of low-calorie Italian

dressing

2 tangerines

Pizza muffin: 1 small whole-wheat English muffin topped with ¼ cup part-skim mozzarella cheese, ½ cup of marinara sauce, 2 slices of zucchini, and 1 oz. of reduced-fat turkey pepperoni. Broiled until cheese melts.

Dinner

Grilled tuna steaks with black sesame seeds

½ cup of stir-fried snow peas

½ cup of mango sorbet

½ cup of cooked udon or soba noodles

Snacks

2 tbsp of hummus on 1 small whole wheat pita bread

6 oz. of tomato juice

Day 7 – Sunday

For today's meal plan, have beans in your diet. Kindly note that the Halibut Salad listed here contains chickpeas that are slowly digested. They help in blood sugar regulation. Additionally, they have excellent protein content with none of the artery-clogging cholesterol or fat seen in many other high-protein items.

Breakfast

½ cup cinnamon-sprinkle cooked sugar-free oatmeal

2 tbsp of raisins

1 cup of free-fat milk

Lunch

Halibut and Chickpea salad

2 small plums

1 oz. of whole-grain crackers

Dinner

½ Cornish game hen, grilled

½ cup honeydew and cantaloupe chunks

½ cooked wild rice

½ cup stir-fried broccoli with red bell pepper (in a wok over high heat, stir-fry in 1 tsp of canola oil

Snacks

1 fruit bar, frozen (all fruit, no sugar)

3 graham crackers (whole wheat)

Week 2 Diabetic Meal Plan

Day 8 – Monday

For today's diet, consider adding blueberries. What makes this fruit special? Antioxidants abound in blueberries, which outnumber those in most other plants. Furthermore, blueberries have a low glycemic index, which is a calculation of how carbs affect blood sugar levels. Low-score foods have little effect on blood sugar levels.

Breakfast

1 slice (1 oz.) of oatmeal bread

½ cup of Blueberry Blast Smoothie

1 tsp of canola margarine

Lunch

½ cup of fresh pineapple chunks

Rice salad and lentil

Cherry tomatoes and zucchini salad (½ cups of tomatoes and zucchinis, 2 tsp of olive oil, and 2 tsp of balsamic vinegar per half)

Dinner

½ cup of cooked quinoa

4 oz. of grilled scallops

½ cup of sliced grapes in a sugar-free, fat-free vanilla yogurt

½ cup of tablespoon red and yellow onion peppers (salt red and ball-bell pepper strips in 1 teaspoon olive oil with slimly cut red onion, sprinkle with ½ teaspoon of dried basil)

Snack

1 cup vegetable soup (low-fat, low-sodium)

1 oz. of reduced-fat string cheese with 1 oz. of whole-grain crackers

Day 9 – Tuesday

How is today coming up with your meal? Are you thinking of spicing things up a bit? Here is what you should know. It is not necessarily important to use a lot of salt, fat, or sugar to make tasty food. Manhattan Clam Chowder is a prime example of this — it tastes much like the cream-based variety but without the sugar and calories.

Breakfast

1 cup of fat-free milk

1 tsp of canola margarine

Salad with mixed berries (1 serving)

1 oz. of whole wheat roll

Lunch

1 slice (1 oz.) of seven-grain bread

Manhattan Clam Chowder

1 cup of mixed field greens salad with 2 tbsp non-fat blue cheese sauce

Dinner

½ cup of brown rice simmered in a low-fat, low-sodium chicken broth

Tomato cucumber salad with grilled chicken

½ cup of snow peas, steamed

½ baked pear (halve and core an unpeeled pear, put cut-side down in the baking dish, pour low-calorie cranberry juice halfway up the sides, bake for 30 to 40 minutes at 375 degrees)

Snacks

½ cup of mango chunks

½ cup of low-fat cottage cheese mixed with 1 tsp of sugar-free jam and ½ tsp of cinnamon

Day 10 – Wednesday

Your meals for today include salad. Concerning that, the apples in Waldorf Salad are rich in pectin, a form of fiber. This "soluble" fiber makes you stay fuller for longer and lowers cholesterol levels. Choosing low-calorie diets that keep you comfortable helps with weight management, which is a problem for many diabetics.

<u>Breakfast</u>

1 tbsp of sugar-free maple syrup

1 small whole-wheat waffle

½ banana

1 oz. of reduced-fat turkey sausage link

Lunch

Waldorf salad

3 oz. low-sodium lean ham slices

1 tsp of canola margarine on ½ toasted English muffin

Dinner

½ cup of sautéed spinach

Turkey Burgers with Tomato Corn Salsa

1 cup cabbage salad (made with ¼ cup of shredded carrots, 2 tbsp of minced onion, and 1 tbsp of low-calorie dressing)

Snacks

1 chocolate pudding (sugar-free, fat-free)

2 tsp of sugar-free jam on ½ small whole-wheat toasted

bagel

Day 11 – Thursday

It is another great day to create a change in your dieting habits. Eating the same meals over and over again not only induces frustration but it can also make losing weight more difficult. People leave their healthier diets based on such frustrations. Using broccolini instead of the more traditional broccoli in the Garlicky Broccolini recipe makes the meal plan that much more exciting.

Breakfast

½ cup of hot wheat cereal

2 tbsp of raisins

¼ cup of grated apple

1 cup of fat-free milk

1 tbsp of sliced toasted almonds

Lunch

1 nectarine

Tabbouleh (with chicken)

1 cup of salad (carrots, cherry tomatoes, butter lettuce, tossed with 2 tbsp of reduced-fat Thousand Island dressing)

Dinner

Garlicky Broccolini

4 oz. of baked halibut fillet

½ cup of chocolate yogurt (sugar-free, fat-free)

1 small (3 oz.) baked potato mixed with chopped chives and 2 tbsp of reduced-fat sour

Snacks

1 oz. of tortilla chips (fat-free)

Salsa

1 oz. of unsalted cashews

Day 12 – Friday

Do you find your meals to be repetitive? With a treat like Peach French Toast Bake, it is time to bring more variety to your diet, and you may forget you are having the best time of your life. It is good to know that you can indulge in some treats, particularly if you can customize them to suit your particular requirements.

Breakfast

1 slice (1 oz.) of Canadian bacon

Peach French toast bake

1 cup of fat-free milk

Lunch

½ cup of fresh cherries

Greek Salad and Oregano chicken, marinated

1 oz. of whole-wheat breadsticks

Dinner

½ cup of kale sautéed in 1 tsp of extra virgin olive oil

1 small ear of corn

Crab cakes

½ cup of fresh raspberries and tbsp of nonfat, sugarless lemon yogurt topping.

Snacks

2 oz. of low-fat turkey slices wrapped in 1 oz. of Swiss cheese (reduced fat)

½ cup of tapioca pudding (nonfat, sugar-free)

Day 13 – Saturday

What are you having for the weekend? Parfait, pita chips, and snow cones? Splash your meals with soups as well. Soup, juices, and vegetables with a high water content make you feel complete and happy while also avoiding overfeeding. The Chicken and Pasta Soup is low in calories, has a lot of flavors, and has a lot of water in both the broth and the vegetables.

Breakfast

1 cup of plain nonfat milk, ½ cup of sliced bananas, and ¼ cup of low-fat granola, layered in a yogurt granola parfait.

Lunch

Chicken and Pasta Soup

3 Fig Newton cookies (whole wheat)

1 cup watercress salad with sliced radishes and 2 tbsp of

low-fat Italian dressing

Dinner

Mango Strawberry Snow Cones

Linguine with Shrimp

½ cup of sautéed broccoli

Snacks

1 oz. of whole-wheat pita chips

6 oz. of carrot juice

Day 14 – Sunday

Fiber and filling are two strengths of whole-wheat pasta, such as the one made with Sicilian-Style Cauliflower. Kindly keep in mind the significance of portion size.

Breakfast

1 oz. of reduced-fat turkey sausage patty

1 cup of fat-free milk

Healthy carrot muffin

Lunch

½ cup of applesauce, topped with ½ tsp of pumpkin pie spice

1 oz. of reduced-fat Swiss cheese, 1 small pita bread (whole-wheat), 1 romaine lettuce leaf, and 3 oz. of canned tuna mixed with celery, 2 tbsp of minced onion, grated carrot, and 2 tbsp of reduced-fat mayonnaise.

Dinner

1 cup of romaine lettuce, zucchini, tomatoes, and 2 tsp of fat-free Caesar dressing tossed together

2 small plums

3 oz. of grilled chicken

Cauliflower in a Sicilian Theme of Whole Wheat Pasta

Snacks

1 tbsp of reduced-fat peanut butter and ½ apple

1 oz. of pretzels (whole wheat)

Week 3 Diabetic Meal Plan

Day 15 – Monday

A new week has begun. How do you keep track of your cholesterol levels? It was once believed that avoiding shellfish was an ideal way to lower cholesterol. However, studies have found that high-saturated-fat diets (rather than dietary cholesterol) impact blood cholesterol levels. The saturated and total fat content of shellfish (as in San Francisco Cioppino) is extremely low. Clams, shrimp, squid, and crab are also excellent choices.

Breakfast

½ cup of fat-free milk

1 vegetarian sausage link

2 (4-inch) whole-wheat pancakes with a topping mixture, comprising 2 tsp of blueberry jam (sugar-free) and ¼ cup of part-skim ricotta cheese

Lunch

½ cup each of yellow and red pepper strips

1 toasted small tortilla (whole-wheat)

½ cup of canned pineapple (water-packed)

Spinach salad and chickpea mixed with yogurt sauce and cumin dressing.

Dinner

1 (1 oz.) slice sourdough bread (whole-wheat)

1 small apple baked in cranberry juice with little calories

San Francisco Cioppino

1 cup of butter lettuce salad tossed with 2 tbsp of non-fat blue cheese sauce, ¼ cup of diced yellow tomato, 2 tsp of gorgonzola cheese, ¼ cup of diced carrot, and ¼ cup of diced zucchini

Snacks

1 oz. of Cheddar cheese wedge (reduced-fat)

½ small baked sweet potato with 2 tsp of maple syrup topping (sugar-free)

Day 16 – Tuesday

Yogurt will become a regular part of your diet as you stick to the 30-day meal schedule. This diet provides a lot of calcium. It has a high protein content and can be used in place of cream and other high-fat foods. It makes a rich, satisfying sauce for the salmon in the Poached Salmon with Lemon Tzatziki, without all the fat in other sauces.

Breakfast

Cheese and tomato omelet comprising ¼ cup of mushrooms (chopped), 3 egg whites, ¼ cup of chopped tomato, 1 oz. of reduced-fat Swiss cheese cooked in 1 tsp of canola margarine or olive oil

½ cup of fresh blackberries

1 (1 oz.) of slice pumpernickel bread

Lunch

½ cup of sliced peaches and mint sprig

3 sesame breadsticks (whole-wheat)

Poached salmon and lemon-mint tzatziki

Dinner

1 small (2 oz.) toasted bun (whole-wheat)

Edamame garden burger

1 cup of red leaf lettuce salad tossed with ½ sliced tomato, ½ cup of diced cucumber, ¼ cup of shredded carrots, and 2 tbsp of French dressing (non-fat)

Snack

2 small fresh apricots

1 cup of milk (fat-free)

Day 17 – Wednesday

You can reduce your saturated fat intake while increasing your fiber intake by consuming naturally low-fat vegan cuisines like beans and grains. Hummus, for example, has a rich flavor without the accompanying guilt.

Breakfast

Apple muffins

½ cup of vegetable soup (low-fat, reduced-sodium)

½ cup of cottage cheese (fat-free), sprinkled with ¼ cup of shredded carrots

Lunch

Vegetarian sandwich comprising ¼ cup of shredded carrots, 3 tbsp of hummus, 2 slices of whole-wheat bread, 2 thin slices of cucumber, and 2 slices of tomato.

½ cup of cantaloupe cubes with a lime wedge

Dinner

½ cup of sliced papaya

½ cup of roasted red potatoes

½ cup of broiled eggplant

Baked Mahi Mahi with wine and herbs

Snacks

1 oz. of part-skim string cheese

Grilled pita triangles

Day 18 – Thursday

You should replace your meals if you crave the flavor of fried foods but are concerned with fats and calories. Crispy Chicken Fingers, which are baked after being wrapped in cereal, have the consistency of fried chicken without the calories.

Breakfast

1 cup of milk (free-fat)

½ sliced banana

½ cup of cooked oatmeal with ¼ tsp of nutmeg and

cinnamon each

Lunch

1 (1 oz.) of sliced Italian bread (whole-wheat)

Minestrone with beans, pasta, and vegetables

3 dried apricot halves

1 cup of romaine lettuce, ½ cup of halved cherry tomatoes, and 1 tsp of Parmesan cheese with 2 tbsp of Caeser dressing (non-fat)

Dinner

½ cup of frozen peach yogurt (sugar-free, fat-free)

Crispy chicken fingers

½ small baked potato with 1 tbsp of tomato salsa topping

Coleslaw made with ½ tsp of poppy seeds, ¼ cup of

shredded carrots, ½ cup of shredded green cabbage, and 2 tbsp of minced red onion, tossed with 2 tsp of apple cider vinegar and 2 tsp of olive oil

Snack

1 rice cake spread with 2 tsp of raspberry jam (sugar-free)

1 oz. of shelled walnuts

Day 19 – Friday

Enjoy your lunch with a splash of Kiwis. The fruit is a very good source of vitamin C, fiber, and potassium (a major antioxidant to prevent heath disease). It provides more than a medium banana potassium

Breakfast

1 tsp of canola margarine

1 small muffin (whole-wheat)

½ cup of lemon yogurt (sugar-free, fat-free) with ½ cup of raspberry topping

Lunch

1 peeled and sliced kiwi

½ toasted English muffin

Slow-roasted salmon with cucumber dill salad

Dinner

1 all-fruit frozen juice bar

½ cup of brown rice cooked in low-sodium chicken broth

Thai style shrimp stir-fry with basil and tomatoes

Snacks

1 oz. of baked tortilla chips (low-fat) and 2 tbsp of salsa

½ apple spread with 2 tsp of peanut butter (reduced-fat)

Day 20 – Saturday

Although it's vital to keep an eye on the amount of fat you consume, it's also crucial to consider consistency. The avocados used in the Chunky Guacamole are high in monounsaturated fat, which is healthy for your cholesterol. Furthermore, avocados contain lutein, a phytochemical that tends to assist in the prevention of age-related macular degeneration. This may be critical for diabetics who are trying to lose weight.

Breakfast

Open-faced egg and tomato sandwich comprising 1 tomato slice, 1 (1 oz.) of turkey slice or 1 slice of cooked Canadian bacon, and 1 poached egg

1 cup of fat-free milk

½ toasted English muffin (whole-wheat)

½ cup of fresh poached figs. Cook the figs in equal

quantities of water and apple juice, sautéed with a clove or two and cinnamon stick until soft, and serve with poaching liquid.

Lunch

4 tortilla chips, baked

1 cup of black bean soup (low-sodium, low-fat) and 1 tbsp of sour cream (low-fat) topping

½ cup of water-packed mandarin oranges

½ cup of carrot sticks dipped in 1 tbsp of Ranch dressing (non-fat)

Dinner

½ cup of cooked couscous (whole-wheat)

Snapper with garlic, roasted grape tomatoes, and basil

3 vanilla sandwich crème cookie (sugar-free)

Spinach salad comprising 1 tbsp of sliced toasted almonds, ¼ sliced mushrooms, 2 red onion slices, 1 cup of spinach leaves, and 2 tbsp of Italian salad dressing (nonfat)

Snacks

1 cup of plain yogurt (nonfat) and 2 tsp of strawberry jam (sugar-free)

1 oz. of crackers (whole-wheat) with 2 tbsp of Chunky Guacamole

Day 21 – Sunday

Are you thinking of making today your cheat day? What meal would you like? Maybe a cup of hot chocolate is not bad for enjoying the weekend. Here is what you should know. Chocolate and other decadent foods are not forbidden. The thick, fluffy hot chocolate is an excellent example of how to eat a limited amount of usually taboo food. Chocolate is just a cup away when combined with low-fat milk and bolstered with sugar-free products.

Breakfast

1 oz. of shredded wheat cereal

½ cup of blueberries

1 oz. of cooked turkey bacon

½ cup of fat-free milk

Lunch

½ cup of applesauce (sugar-free) with ¼ tsp of ground ginger

1 small whole-grain roll with 1 tsp of canola oil margarine

Chopped niçoise salad

Dinner

½ cup of fusilli pasta (whole-wheat)

½ cup of peach sprinkled with 2 tsp of unsweetened toasted coconut

Chicken cacciatore

½ cup of sautéed broccolini with 1 tbsp of toasted pine nut topping

<u>Snacks</u>

1 oz. of pretzels (whole-wheat) and Dijon mustard

Hot chocolate

Week 4 Diabetic Meal Plan

Day 22 – Monday

Have you considered baking instead of frying? Oven-Baked Parmesan French Fries are a fantastic way to get the crunch of fried foods without any of the sugar and calories.

Breakfast

1 egg (scrambled) in 1 tsp of olive oil, with 1 tsp of chopped chives topping

Applegurt (½ serving)

Lunch

1 orange

½ whole-wheat bagel spread with 2 tsp of cream cheese (reduced-fat)

Raspberry chicken salad

Dinner

5 asparagus spears (grilled)

Oven-baked Parmesan French fries

4 oz. of grilled beef tenderloin

10 red grapes

Mixed tomato salad – includes ¼ cup of halved cherry tomatoes, ½ cup of cubed red tomatoes, 2 tsp of minced fresh basil, and 2 tbsp of chopped Vidalia onion, drizzled with 2 tsp of balsamic vinegar

Snacks

½ cup of edamame

1 oz. of roasted unsalted cashews

Day 23 – Tuesday

Should pumpkins figure prominently in your today's menu? Of course, they should. This variety of squash contains beta carotene, a safe antioxidant that can help prevent disease. Pumpkin muffins made from canned pumpkin have the same nutritional value as whole pumpkins.

Breakfast

1 cup of milk (fat-free)

Pumpkin muffins

Lunch

½ cup of vanilla pudding (fat-free, sugar-free)

½ cup of tomato soup (low-fat, reduced-sodium)

Crab salad sandwich – includes 3 oz. of cooked crabmeat with ¼ cup of chopped red pepper, 1 tbsp of mayonnaise (low-fat), ½ tsp of capers, ¼ cup of chopped celery, placed in a pita pocket (whole-wheat) with lettuce or spinach

Dinner

½ cooked artichoke dipped in a mixture comprising 1 tbsp of mayonnaise (low-fat) and ¼ tsp of lemon zest

Garlic lime chicken

2 plums

½ cup of cooked orzo (whole-wheat)

Snack

6 oz. of blueberry yogurt (fat-free, sugar-free)

½ banana spread with 1 tsp of almond butter

Day 24 – Wednesday

Your meal will not be complete without Pomegranates. These fruits are high in vitamin C, potassium, and fiber and are low in calories. They also contain ellagic, anthocyanins, and tannins acids, all of which are strong antioxidants that can help prevent heart disease.

Breakfast

1 egg fried in 1 tsp of olive oil

1 (1 oz.) of slice rye bread

½ cup of sliced strawberries with ½ cup of plain yogurt

Lunch

Pumpernickel ham and watercress sandwich

1 small orange

½ cup of blanched broccoli and cauliflower, each dipped in 2 tbsp of blue cheese dressing (non-fat)

Dinner

½ cup of sautéed spinach

1 cup of salad tossed with 2 tbsp of Thousand Island dressing (nonfat)

Pork Au Poivre

Ginger tea cake

Snacks

½ cup of pomegranate seeds

1 oz. of pretzels (whole-wheat)

Day 25 – Thursday

It is vital to integrate a range of textures into your diet. The smooth, creamy texture and crisp crust of this low-calorie, low-fat Banana Cream Pie will satisfy your palate while keeping your waistline trim.

Breakfast

1 cup of milk (fat-free)

¼ cup of chopped dried apples

½ cup of hot seven-grain cereal

Lunch

1 small pita bread (whole-wheat), warmed

Chicken kebabs

10 green grapes

½ cup of sautéed portobello mushrooms, cooked in 1 tsp of olive oil

Dinner

3 oz. of grilled salmon

½ cup of brown rice cooked in chicken broth (reduced-sodium)

Grilled salad with herbed vinaigrette

Banana cream pie (1 serving)

Snack

6 oz. of tomato juice (low-sodium)

1 hard-boiled egg

Day 26 – Friday

As previously mentioned, your greens should be black. Iceberg lettuce, for example, is a light-colored green that is low in nutrients. Beta carotene, fiber, and iron abound in the chard used in Seared Greens with Red Onion and Vinegar.

Breakfast

1 rice cake with 2 tsp of cashew butter

Strawberry and tofu smoothie

Lunch

Spicy bean soup

4 dried plums

3 sesame breadsticks (whole-wheat)

½ cup of halved grape tomatoes and ½ cup of sliced

English cucumber drizzled with 2 tsp of balsamic vinegar

Dinner

3 oz. of baked tilapia

1 cup of tossed salad drizzled with 2 tsp of herb vinegar and 1 tsp of walnut oil.

½ cup of barley cooked in chicken broth (reduced-sodium)

Seared greens with red onion and vinegar

Snacks

½ cup of cottage cheese (low-fat) with 1 tsp of toasted slivered almonds

½ cup of mixed fruit salad (water-packed)

Day 27 – Saturday

Add beets to your meal today. They are low in calories

and rich in folate, vitamin C, and potassium, which are both heart-healthy nutrients. Even though beets have a higher carbohydrate content than many other vegetables, diabetics can consume them. Enjoy the guilt-free Beet and Mandarin Orange Salad with Mint.

Breakfast

½ cup of sliced star fruit or carambola

½ bagel (whole-wheat) with 1 oz. of melted Jarlsberg cheese (reduced-fat)

Lunch

1 small roll (whole-grain)

3 oz. of grilled shrimp

1 tsp of canola margarine

Beet and mandarin orange salad with mint

Dinner

½ cup of frozen vanilla yogurt (fat-free, sugar-free)

Sautéed Green Beans and Pimento

Spaghetti (whole-wheat) with Pecorino cheese and Swiss chard

Snacks

1 oz. of lean turkey breast

2 cups of air-popped popcorn

Day 28 – Sunday

Tofu is a low-saturated-fat, high-protein vegetarian alternative for your meal schedule. Tofu's ability to digest any flavor you add is one of its strongest qualities; in Wok-Sautéed tofu and Mushrooms, for example, the former takes on an Asian taste.

Breakfast

1 cup of milk (fat-free)

3 egg whites, scrambled in 1 tsp of olive oil and topped with 1 tsp of chopped basil and 1 tbsp of Cheddar cheese(reduced-fat)

Blueberry compote

Lunch

Open-face lean roast beef sandwich, comprising a mixture of 1 romaine lettuce leaf, 3 oz. of lean roast beef, 2 tsp of Dijon honey mustard, 1 slice whole-grain, and green apple, carrot, and mint salad

Dinner

½ cup of cooked soba noodles

½ cup of honeydew chunks sprinkled with 1 tsp of minced crystallized ginger

Wok-Sautéed Mushrooms and Tofu

Snacks

2 tbsp of bean dip (low-fat) with 1 oz. of baked tortilla chips

6 oz. of raspberry yogurt (non-fat, sugar-free)

Week 5 Diabetic Meal Plan

Day 29 – Monday

You have one more day to conclude the meal schedule. Look for 120 grams of carbohydrates a day, which comprises 34 grams at breakfast, 40 grams at lunch, and 34 grams at dinner. Snacks for the day could produce 12 calories. Enjoy tasty recipes like the veggie omelet, salmon, and succotash while you are at it.

Breakfast

¾ cup of blueberries

Two-egg veggie omelet – includes mushrooms, spinach, avocado, and bell pepper

Lunch

1 tbsp of plain Greek yogurt (nonfat) and 1 tbsp of mustard

Two regular slices of whole-grain bread (high-fiber)

1 cup of sliced tomato, 2 oz. of canned tuna (water-packed) with ¼ cup of shredded carrots

½ medium apple

1 tbsp of dill relish

Dinner

½ cup of succotash (50g)

2 oz. of pork tenderloin

1 tsp of butter

½ cup of fresh pineapple

1 cup of cooked asparagus

Snacks

1 cup of unsweetened kefir

Day 30 – Tuesday

As the last day of your meal schedule arrives, it's important to focus on your success and the outcomes you've accomplished. Consider yogurt, potatoes, tofu, broccoli, and berries for today's meal. Also, rather than frying your food, bake or toast it.

Breakfast

Sweet potato toast, comprising 2 slices of toasted sweet potato (100g) with 1 tsp of sprinkled flaxseed, spinach, and 1 oz. goat cheese for topping

Lunch

1 cup of fresh strawberries

1 cup of raw cauliflower

2 oz. of roast chicken

1 tbsp of French dressing (low-fat)

Dinner

8 oz. of silken tofu

2/3 cup of quinoa

1 cup of steamed broccoli

1 cup of cooked bok choy

1 kiwi

2 tsp of olive oil

Snacks

1 cup of plain Greek yogurt (low-fat) and ½ banana

Diabetes Meal Recipes for Breakfast

Following a diabetes meal schedule will assist you in fulfilling your everyday dietary requirements. It may also have variety and, if desired, aid in weight loss. A diabetes meal schedule will also help you keep track of carbohydrates and calories while also adding variety to your diet by incorporating fresh concepts. There is no one-size-fits-all strategy that would work for everybody. Finally, you can see a doctor or a dietitian to devise a meal schedule. Check to see if the amounts are right or if they need to be changed. Measuring meal servings will help you keep track of your diet and dietary consumption. This guide has balanced each food group to create the optimal eating schedule to give you the perfect morning diet.

The most critical meal of the day is breakfast. This is likely even more true for diabetics. A morning meal will help you maintain a healthy blood sugar level during the day. It was discovered in one study that missing it resulted in higher blood sugar spikes during lunch and dinner.

Breakfasts, on the other hand, are not always made equal. Breakfast can contain fiber, lean protein, and good fats to help you get the day off correctly. This section's recipes are based on the meal plan from the previous section. The majority of the meals mentioned previously, as well as guidance on how to cook them, can be found here. It also contains additional meals to widen your options.

1/2 recipe Blueberry Blast Smoothie

The preparation time for this meal is 2 – 3 minutes. The nutritional value per serving for this smoothie is as follows:

Calories: 194 calorie

Total fat: 1 gram

Saturated fat: 0 gram

Cholesterol: 5 milligrams

Sodium: 133 milligrams

Carbohydrate: 40 grams

Dietary fiber: 4 grams

Ingredients

½ cup of nonfat plain yogurt

1 cup of frozen blueberries (unsweetened)

½ cup of nonfat or 1 percent low-fat milk

1 tsp of honey

Preparation

Pour all the ingredients into a blender and blend until smooth.

Mixed Berry Salad

This salad includes high-fiber fruits as well as a small amount of yogurt. Apples, pears, blackberries, cherries, peaches, plums, and grapes are few other fruits that may be included. It takes just 15 minutes to cook and serves one to two people. The difficulty level is set to medium. To enjoy your mixed berry salad in moderation, you need to know its nutritional value, which is listed below per serving:

Calories: 60 calorie

Total fat: 0.5 grams

Saturated fat: 0 grams

Cholesterol: 1 milligram

Sodium: 24 milligrams

Carbohydrates: 13 grams

Dietary fiber: 2.5 grams

Protein: 2 grams

Sugar: 10 grams

Ingredients

Juice of ½ lime or 1 tbsp

2 tbsp of yogurt (low-fat) (try lemon or key-lime)

1 tbsp of fresh mint leaves, torn

1 cup of cubed cantaloupe

¼ cup of raspberries

¼ cup of blueberries

4 medium strawberries, stemmed and quartered

Preparation

In a medium mixing cup, add the yogurt, lime juice, and mint. Toss in the fruit to blend. Serve.

Applegurt

The preparation time for this meal is 3 minutes, and the cooking time is 20 minutes. It serves 1 person. Applegurt comes with the following nutritional value per serving:

Calories: 292 calorie

Total fat: 2.4 grams

Saturated fat: 1 gram

Carbohydrates: 62 grams

Dietary fiber: 4 grams

Protein: 9.3 grams

Ingredients

½ cup of plain yogurt

½ cup of unsweetened applesauce

1 tbsp of honey

½ cup of granola or whole-grain cereal

Preparation

Combine the yogurt, applesauce, and honey in a mixing

bowl. Enable 20 minutes for chilling. Granola should be sprinkled on top.

Apple Muffins

It is worth noting that this apple muffin recipe serves 12 persons. It takes 15 minutes to prepare the ingredients and 40 minutes to cook. The setting should be placed at "easy." The list below shows the nutritional value of this meal per serving:

Calories: 216 calorie

Total fat: 7.5 grams

Saturated fat: 1 gram

Cholesterol: 32 milligrams

Sodium: 234 milligrams

Dietary fiber: 2 grams

Carbohydrates: 34 grams

Sugar: 20 grams

Protein: 4 grams

Ingredients

Nonstick cooking spray

¾ cup plus 2 tbsp of packed brown sugar

¼ cup of chopped pecans

½ tsp of ground cinnamon

1 cup of all-purpose flour

1 tsp of baking soda

1 cup of whole-wheat pastry flour

2 large eggs

¼ cup of canola oil

½ tsp of fine salt

1 tsp of vanilla extract

1 cup of natural applesauce

¾ cup of low-fat buttermilk

1 golden apple, peeled, cored, and cut into ¼-inch pieces

Preparation

1. Preheat oven to 400 degrees Fahrenheit. Spray a 12-cup standard muffin pan with nonstick cooking spray.

2. Combine the pecans, 2 teaspoons of brown sugar, and the cinnamon in a small bowl.

3. Whisk together the all-purpose and whole wheat flour, baking soda, and salt in a medium mixing cup.

4. Whisk together the remaining ¾ cup of sugar and the oil in a large mixing bowl. One at a time, add the eggs, whisking well after each inclusion. Combine the applesauce and vanilla extract in a mixing cup.

5. In two batches, whisk in the flour mixture, mixing with the buttermilk. Only mix all with a whisk. Stir in the apple pieces softly.

6. Sprinkle the pecan mixture over the batter in the prepared muffin pan. To remove any air bubbles, tap the pan on the counter a few times. Bake for 20 to 25 minutes, or until a wooden pick inserted in the center of one of the muffins comes out clean.

7. Enable 15 minutes for cooling on a wire rack. To remove and unmold the muffins, run a knife through them. Enable to cool absolutely on a shelf.

Strawberry and Tofu Smoothie

Strawberry and tofu smoothie takes about 10 minutes to prepare. This recipe serves 4 persons, 6 ounces each. The setting is left at "easy." The nutritional value per serving includes:

Calories: 140 calorie

Total fat: 12 grams

Saturated fat: 7 grams

Carbohydrates: 7 grams

Dietary fiber: 2 grams

Ingredients

1 cup of frozen strawberries (if using new berries, freeze them first, don't defrost)

1 cup of ice

1 cup of ice water

½ cup of heavy cream (to lighten up, substitute water)

¼ cup of sugar substitute (recommended: Splenda)

3 (½ oz.) soft or silken tofu

½ teaspoon vanilla extract (There should be no sugar in the ingredients list)

Preparation

1. Prepare the Smoothie: In a blender, combine all of the ingredients and pulse to slice them up. Increase the speed to fast and blend until almost smooth.

2. Pour the smoothie into four cups and finish with a strawberry and a mint sprig in each.

Blueberry Compote

It takes 5 minutes to prepare this meal and 18 minutes to cook. You can get ½ cup (8 servings) from this recipe. Set the level to "easy." Here is the nutritional value for each serving:

Calories: 44 calorie

Sodium: 0.4 milligrams

Dietary fiber: 1 gram

Carbohydrates: 11 grams

Ingredients

3 tbsp of water

2 cups of frozen blueberries

¼ cup of sugar

2 teaspoons of lemon juice

Preparation

In a shallow saucepan, combine 1 cup of blueberries, water, sugar, and lemon juice. Cook for around 10 minutes over medium heat. Cook for another 8 minutes, stirring constantly, after adding the rest of the blueberries. Heat the dish before serving.

Peach French Toast Bake

It takes 5 minutes to prepare this meal and 18 minutes to cook. You can get ½ cup (8 servings) from this recipe. Set the level to "easy." For each serving, you get the following:

Calories: 267 calorie

Cholesterol: 144 milligrams

Carbohydrates: 44 grams

Protein: 13 grams

Dietary fiber 5 grams

Saturated fats: 1.5 grams

Total fats: 6 grams

Sodium: 288 milligrams

Ingredients

Nonstick cooking spray

1 large baguette (about 8 oz.) (whole-wheat)

4 whole eggs

4 egg whites

1 tsp of vanilla extract

1 cup milk (low-fat)

5 cups of sliced peaches, fresh or frozen

3 tbsp of brown sugar

¼ tsp of ground cinnamon

½ lemon, juiced about 1 ½ tbsp

Preparation

1. Spray a 9 by a 13-inch baking pan with cooking spray. Break the baguette into ½-inch slices and place the slices in a single layer in the baking pan.

2. Combine the eggs, egg whites, sugar, and vanilla extract in a mixing bowl. Over the bread in the pan, pour the egg mixture.

3. Toss peaches with lemon juice and 1 tablespoon brown sugar in a medium mixing cup. Arrange the peach slices on top of the bread in an even layer. Sprinkle the rest of the brown sugar and cinnamon over the top. Refrigerate overnight, covered.

4. Preheat oven to 350 degrees Fahrenheit. Bake for 40 minutes after removing the cover.

Healthy Carrot Muffin

Servings for this recipe amount to 12 persons. You need 15 minutes to prepare the ingredients and 30 minutes to cook. The setting stays at "easy." This healthy carrot muffin contains 179 calories per serving. Other details include:

Saturated fats: 1 gram

Total fats: 7 grams

Sodium: 110 milligrams

Cholesterol: 31 milligrams

Sugar: 14 grams

Protein: 3 grams

Ingredients

½ cup of flour (whole-wheat)

¾ cup of all-purpose flour

2/3 cup of dark brown sugar

2 large eggs

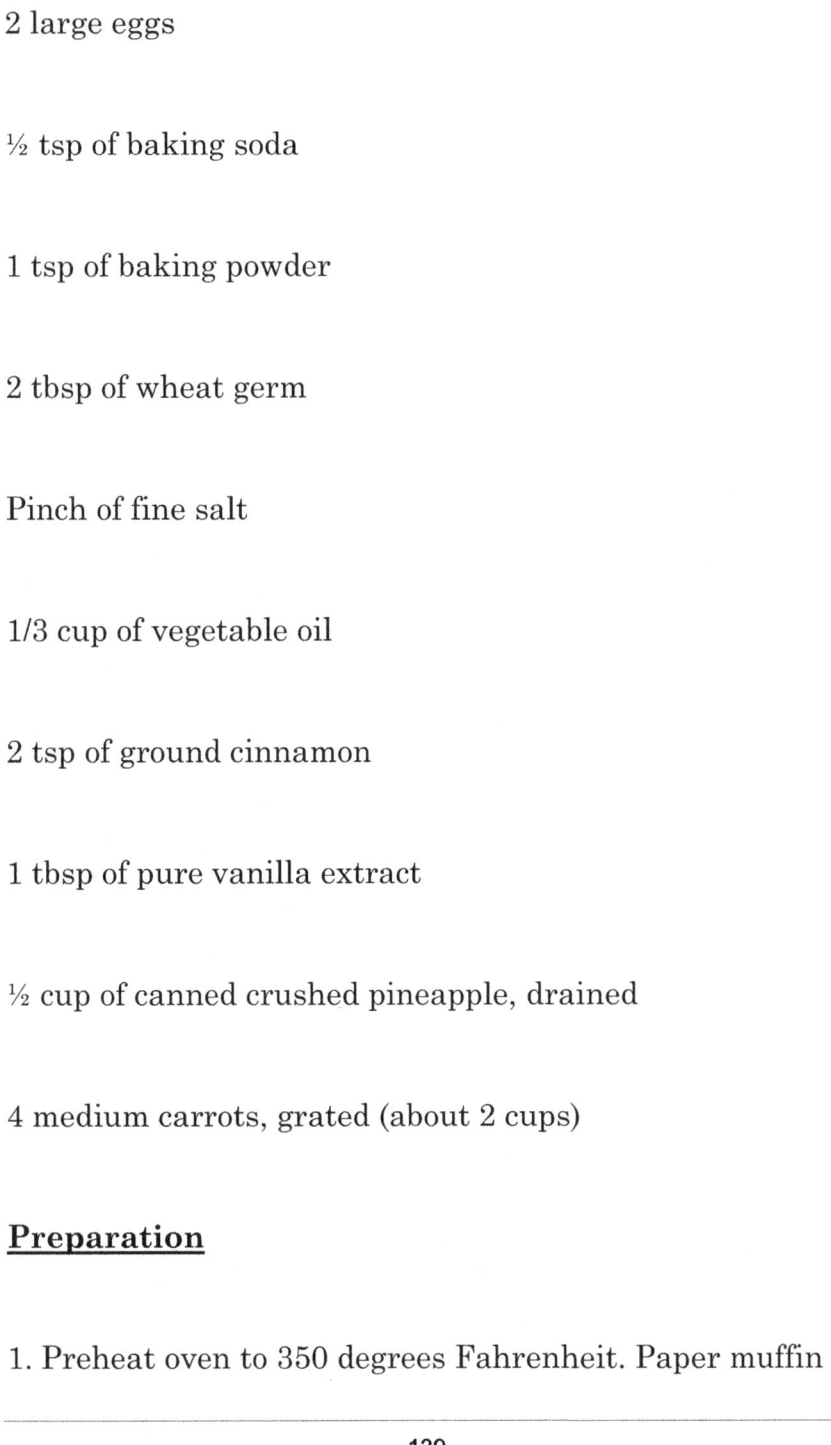

½ tsp of baking soda

1 tsp of baking powder

2 tbsp of wheat germ

Pinch of fine salt

1/3 cup of vegetable oil

2 tsp of ground cinnamon

1 tbsp of pure vanilla extract

½ cup of canned crushed pineapple, drained

4 medium carrots, grated (about 2 cups)

Preparation

1. Preheat oven to 350 degrees Fahrenheit. Paper muffin

liners can be used to fill twelve ½-cup muffin cups.

2. In a medium mixing cup, combine the flours, brown sugar, wheat germ, cinnamon, baking powder, baking soda, and salt. Lightly whisk the egg in a separate medium dish, then add the vegetable oil and vanilla extract.

3. Quickly and lightly fold the wet ingredients into the dry ingredients using a rubber spatula. Stir in the carrots and pineapple only before evenly moist; the batter would be very thick. Evenly spread the batter among the muffin cups. Bake for 30 minutes, or until golden and a toothpick inserted in the center comes out clean. Remove the muffins from the pans and set them to cool on a wire rack. Heat the dish before eating.

Bagel Avocado Toast

In one nutritious meal, combine the flavor of a bagel with the creaminess of avocado toast. When you need to get out the door quickly, simply toast, top, and sprinkle for this simple morning breakfast. If you need to spice it up a little, add a poached or fried egg on top. It takes 5 minutes to prepare this toast and serves 1 person.

Calories: 172 calorie

Carbohydrates: 17.8 grams

Cholesterol: 31 milligrams

Protein: 5.4 grams

Dietary fiber: 5.9 grams

Fat: 9.8 grams

Saturated fat: 1.4 grams

Sugar: 2.3 grams

Dietary fiber: 5.9 grams

Vitamins A (73.71IU), C (5.5 milligrams)

Folate: 63mcg

Calcium: 60.5 milligrams

Added sugar: 1 gram

Thiamine: 0.1 milligram

Sodium: 251.8 milligrams

Magnesium: 41.4 milligram

Iron: 1.3 milligram

Potassium: 341.5 milligrams

Exchanges: 2 Fat, 1 Starch

Ingredients

1 sliced toasted bread (whole-grain)

¼ medium avocado, mashed

2 tsp of bagel seasoning

Pinch of flaky sea salt, such as Maldon

Preparation

Spread avocado on toast and add seasoning alongside salt.

Healthy Carrot Muffins

Servings for this recipe amount to 12 persons. You need 15 minutes to prepare the ingredients and 30 minutes to cook. The setting stays at "easy." This healthy carrot muffin contains 179 calories per serving. Other details include:

Saturated fats: 1 gram

Total fats: 7 grams

Sodium: 110 milligrams

Cholesterol: 31 milligrams

Sugar: 14 grams

Protein: 3 grams

Ingredients

½ cup of flour (whole-wheat)

¾ cup of all-purpose flour

1/4 teaspoons baking powder

1/2 teaspoon salt

1/3 cup whole milk

1 large egg

2 tablespoons vegetable oil

2 tablespoons brown sugar

1 medium carrot, sliced

1 tsp cinnamon

1 capful of vanilla extract

Preparation

1. Preheat the oven to 350°F (180°C). Line 12 (½-cup) muffin cups with paper muffin liners.

2. In a medium mixing cup, combine the flour, brown sugar, cinnamon, baking powder, baking soda, and salt. Lightly whisk the egg in a separate medium dish, then add the vegetable oil and vanilla extract.

3. Fold the wet ingredients (quickly and lightly) into the dry ingredients using a rubber spatula. Add carrots and stir until evenly moist and the batter becomes thick.

4. Evenly distribute the batter among the muffin cups. Bake for 30 minutes, or until golden and a toothpick inserted in the center comes out clean. Turn muffins out of the tins and cool on a rack. Serve warm.

Lemon Bread

This moist lemon bread is a delicious breakfast or dessert choice. It's perfect on its own or with the added lemon-sugar glaze on top. It takes 30 minutes to prepare its ingredients and a total time of 1 hour, 25 minutes to have it ready. For this recipe, you will get 16 servings. Below shows the meal's nutritional value per serving:

Calories: 140 calorie

Iron: 0.8 milligram

Sodium: 80.3 milligrams

Cholesterol: 0.3 milligrams

Carbohydrates: 21.4 grams

Protein: 2.9 grams

Calcium: 40.5 milligrams

Magnesium: 12.7 milligrams

Potassium: 65.9 milligrams

Dietary fiber: 0.8 grams

Sugars: 10.4 grams

Fat: 5 grams

Saturated fat: 0.5 grams

Vitamin C: 0.8 milligrams

Vitamin A: 78.51IU

Folate: 42.1mcg

Exchanges: 1 ½ another carbohydrate, 1 fat

Ingredients

1 ¾ cups of all-purpose flour

¾ cup of sugar or a sugar replacement mix that equals ¾ sugar (optional)

2 tsp of finely shredded lemon peel

1 cup of nonfat milk

2 tsp of baking powder

¼ cup of cooking oil or melted butter

¼ cup of refrigerated or frozen egg product, thawed, or 1 slightly beaten egg

¼ tsp of salt

1 tbsp of sugar (optional)

2 tbsp of lemon juice (optional)

½ cup of chopped toasted almonds or walnuts

Preparation

1. Preheat the oven to 350 degrees Fahrenheit. Place aside an 8x4x2-inch loaf pan that has been greased on the bottom and 1/2 inch up the sides. Combine flour, 3/4 cup sugar, baking powder, and salt in a medium mixing dish. Make a well in the flour mixture and set it aside.

2. Combine the egg, milk, grease, lemon peel, and 1 tablespoon lemon juice in a separate medium mixing cup. Add the egg mixture to the flour mixture all at once.

3. Stir only until the mixture is moistened (batter should be lumpy). Combine the nuts and fold them in. Pour the batter into the pan that has been packed.

4. Preheat oven to 350°F and bake for 45–55 minutes, or until a wooden toothpick inserted near the middle comes out clean. Combine the 2 tablespoons of lemon juice and 1 tablespoon of sugar, if needed. Brush the lemon-sugar mixture over the top of the loaf while it is still in the pan. Cool for 10 minutes in the pan on a wire rack. Remove the pan from the heat. On a wire stand, cool absolutely. Wrap the dish in plastic wrap and store it in the refrigerator overnight before consumption.

5. There are a few other parts of this recipe worth mentioning. When toasting the whole nuts or big bits, spread them out on parchment paper in a shallow baking tray. Bake for 5 to 10 minutes, or until golden, at 350 degrees F, shaking pan once or twice. For sugar substitutes, it is ideal to use Splenda®. It performs excellently when baking. Directions and a dietary overview are included with this package. You should use only ¾ cup of sugar. The following values can be obtained: fiber (1 gram), calories (126 cal.), carbohydrates (17 grams), and exchanges (1 other carb).

Spinach and Egg Scramble with Raspberries

One of the best breakfasts for weight loss is this short egg scramble with hearty toast. It mixes weight-loss superfoods, eggs, and raspberries, with filling whole-grain toast and nutrient-dense spinach for a filling meal. The protein and fiber in the meal keep you full, and the overall calorie count is just under 300. This recipe takes 10 minutes to prepare and serves 1 person. The following contains the values you get from the meal per serving (1 slice of bread and 2 eggs with ½ cup of raspberries)

Calories: 296 calorie

Dietary fiber: 7 grams

Carbohydrates: 20.9 grams

Protein: 17.8 grams

Saturated fat: 3.7 grams

Fat: 15.7 grams

Sugars: 4.8 grams

Vitamin A: 3312.6IU

Vitamin C: 28.1 milligram

Cholesterol: 372 milligrams

Thiamine: 0.1 milligram

Sodium: 394.2 milligrams

Iron: 4.2 milligrams

Calcium: 138.8 milligrams

Folate: 79.4mcg

Magnesium: 76.1 milligrams

Potassium: 292.6 milligrams

Exchanges: ½ fruit, 1 fat, 2 medium-fat protein, ½ vegetables, and ½ starch

Ingredients

2 large, lightly beaten eggs

1 ½ cups of baby spinach (1 ½ oz.)

1 tsp of canola oil

Pinch of ground pepper

Pinch of kosher salt

½ cup of fresh raspberries

1 slice of toasted bread (whole-grain)

Preparation

Heat oil in a small nonstick skillet over medium-high heat. Add spinach and cook until wilted, stirring often, 1 to 2 minutes. Transfer the spinach to a plate. Wipe the pan clean, place over medium heat, and add eggs. Cook, stirring once or twice to ensure even cooking until just set, 1 to 2 minutes. Stir in the spinach, salt, and pepper. Serve the scramble with toast and raspberries.

Baked Banana-Nut Oatmeal

These fluffy, delicious grab-and-go oatmeal cups combine muffins and oatmeal. You may use some other nut in place of the pecans, such as walnuts, or leave them out entirely. Create a large batch on the weekend and put it in the fridge or freezer for weekday breakfasts. Heat for about 40 seconds in the microwave. The average preparation time for this recipe is 15 minutes, while the cooking time takes about 35 minutes. It serves 12 persons. Here are the nutritional values per serving:

Calories: 176 calorie

Dietary fiber: 3.1 grams

Protein: 5.2 grams

Carbohydrates: 26.4 grams

Sugars: 10.5 grams

Fat: 6.2 grams

Saturated fat: 1.2 grams

Calcium: 85.3 milligrams

Folate: 20.2mcg

Vitamin C: 1.8 milligrams

Cholesterol: 33.4 milligrams

Vitamin A: 118.7IU

Potassium: 227.9 milligrams

Magnesium: 36 milligrams

Iron: 1.1 milligrams

Thiamine: 0.1 milligram

Sodium: 165.6 milligrams

Added sugar: 6 grams

Exchanges: 1 starch, 1 fat, ½ fruit, and ½ another carbohydrate

Ingredients

3 cups of rolled oats

1 ½ cups of low-fat milk

2 ripe bananas, mashed (about ¾ cup)

1/3 cup of packed brown sugar

2 large eggs, lightly beaten

1 tsp of vanilla extract

1 tsp of ground cinnamon

1 tsp of baking powder

½ cup of toasted chopped pecans

½ tsp of salt

Preparation

Preheat the oven to 375 degrees Fahrenheit. Using

cooking oil, coat a muffin dish.

In a big mixing cup, combine the oats, cream, bananas, brown sugar, eggs, baking powder, cinnamon, vanilla, and salt. Add pecans and fold them in. Fill each muffin cup with around 1/3 cup of the mixture. Bake for about 25 minutes, or until a toothpick inserted in the middle comes out clean. Cool for 10 minutes in the pan before removing it to a wire rack to cool out. Warm or room temperature are also suitable serving choices.

Mediterranean Breakfast Sandwich

Do you want a delicious veggie-packed breakfast sandwich? Say no more. On low-carbohydrate sandwich bread, the Mediterranean breakfast sandwich has a good serving of protein and fresh vegetables. It takes 5 mins to prepare and 15 minutes to cook. With this recipe, you can serve 4 people. It contains the following nutritional facts:

Calories: 242 calorie

Protein: 13 grams

Carbohydrates: 25 grams dietary

Fiber: 6.2 grams

Sugars: 3.2 grams

Fat: 11.7 grams

Saturated fat: 2.9 grams

Cholesterol: 214 milligrams

Vitamin A: 2448.4IU

Vitamin C: 12 milligrams

Folate: 28.7mcg

Calcium: 123.2 milligrams

Iron: 3 milligram

Magnesium: 9.9 milligrams

Potassium: 143.8 milligrams

Sodium: 501.2 milligrams

Exchanges: 1 fat, 1 ½ starch, 1 medium-fat protein, and ½ vegetables

Ingredients

4 multigrain sandwich thins

4 tsp of olive oil

1 tbsp of snipped fresh rosemary or ½ tsp of dried rosemary, crushed

2 cups of fresh baby spinach leaves

4 tbsp of feta cheese (reduced-fat)

4 eggs

1 medium tomato, cut into 8 thin slices

Freshly ground black pepper

1/8 teaspoon of kosher salt

Preparation

1. Preheat the oven to 375 degrees Fahrenheit. Brush cut sides of sandwich thins with 2 teaspoons olive oil. Place on a baking sheet and toast for 5 minutes, or until light brown and crisp around the edges.

2. In a large skillet over medium-high heat, heat the remaining 2 teaspoons olive oil and rosemary. In a pan, crack one egg at a time. Cook for 1 minute, or until the whites are firm, but the yolks are still runny. With a spatula, break the yolks. Cook until the eggs are set on the other side. Switch off the burner.

3. Assemble four serving plates by placing the bottom half of the toasted sandwich thins on them. On bowls, divide the spinach among the sandwich thins. Place two tomato strips, an egg, and 1 tablespoon feta cheese on top of each. Season to taste with salt and pepper. Finish with the remaining thin sandwich halves.

Blueberry-Lemon Crumb Muffins

This recipe is for you if you're looking for the right combination of fruits to use in making delectable, light, and airy muffins. Include a crumble of delicate brown sugar. Using lemon extract instead of vanilla if you want a stronger lemon flavor. Fresh blueberries are better in these muffins, though frozen blueberries can be used instead. They don't need to be thawed before being added to the batter. Listed below are details on its nutritional value:

Calories: 197 calorie

Protein: 4.1 grams

Dietary fiber: 1.8 grams

Carbohydrates: 31 grams

Saturated fat: 0.8 grams

Sugars: 14.7 grams

Fat: 6.9 grams

Cholesterol: 31.6 grams

Vitamin A: 62.5IU

Vitamin C: 2.8 milligram

Calcium: 48.6 milligrams

Iron: 2.1 milligrams

Folate: 24.9mcg

Potassium: 74.8 milligrams

Magnesium: 6.3 milligrams

Sodium: 180.9 milligrams

Thiamine: 0.1 milligram

Added sugar: 12 grams

Ingredients

¾ cup of all-purpose flour

1 cup of white flour (whole-wheat)

¼ tsp of baking soda

1 tsp of baking powder

2 large eggs

¼ tsp of salt

1 tbsp of freshly grated lemon zest

½ cup of light brown sugar

¾ cup of buttermilk (low-fat)

3 tbsp of canola oil

1 tsp of lemon extract or vanilla extract

1 ½ cups of fresh or frozen (not thawed) blueberries

Preparation

1. Preheat the oven to 400 degrees Fahrenheit. Using paper liners or cooking oil, fill a 12-cup muffin tray with muffin cups.

2. To make the crumb topping, combine ¼ cup flour, ¼ cup brown sugar, 1 teaspoon of lemon zest, and 1/8 teaspoon of salt in a deep mixing bowl. Stir in 2 teaspoons of oil until crumbly. Put the bowl aside.

3. To make muffins, follow these steps: In a medium mixing dish, combine whole wheat flour, all-purpose flour, baking powder, baking soda, and salt. In a separate medium mixing cup, whisk together the eggs and brown sugar until well combined. Whisk in the buttermilk, grease, lemon zest, and vanilla (or lemon) extract until well mixed.

4. Create a well in the middle of the dry ingredients and add in the wet; mix until just mixed. Stir in the blueberries once just mixed. Divide the batter evenly

between the muffin cups. Sprinkle with the crumb topping and press softly to stick.

5. Bake the muffins for 20 minutes, or until golden brown and a wooden skewer inserted into the center comes out clean. Allow cooling in the pan for 10 minutes before transferring to a wire rack to cool for at least 5 minutes until serving.

Diabetes Meal Recipes for Lunch

Finding the perfect diabetic lunch meal can be difficult. Often, this is the moment that you are cooped up at work and have no access to healthy food. Worse, you are surrounded by a plethora of toxic junk foods, which may aggravate the diabetic disorder. As a result, you must schedule ahead of time so that you have a range of balanced foods to pick from at lunchtime.

This segment includes a variety of cold lunches. Any of

these dishes can be made ahead of time and then reheated at a later date. A few of them need cooking at lunchtime.

You do not need to stress because the recipes in this segment are relatively low in calories, taste delicious, and will give you a balanced energy boost for the afternoon. Your meals should have no more than 20 grams of carbohydrate on average. Choose low glycemic index (GI) meals of at least 20 grams of protein. Here are some diabetic lunch meals to add to your plate.

Spring Vegetable and Herbed Chicken Soup

This sumptuous meal can spice up your lunch breaks and prepare you for the remaining tasks. Preparing the ingredients takes 15 minutes and cooking 30 minutes. It provides 4 to 6 servings.

Ingredients

1 tsp of fennel seeds

¼ cup of chopped fresh parsley leave

¼ cup of chopped fresh thyme leaves

¼ tsp of red pepper flakes

3 cloves of garlic (minced)

Kosher salt

Freshly ground black pepper

3 bone-in, skin-on thighs

3 boneless, skin-on chicken breasts

1 tbsp of butter

3 tbsp of olive oil

cipollini onions, trimmed and peeled

1 cup of chicken broth

8 oz. baby carrots, peeled and trimmed, but with a green tip

6 oz. of snap peas, trimmed

4 oz. of morel mushrooms

Preparation

1. Preheat the oven to 375°F. In a shallow bowl, add the thyme, garlic, pepper, fennel seeds, red pepper flakes, parsley, and a pinch of salt. Stir to combine. Set the chicken parts on a platform and loosen the skins gently. Garnish the inner parts with a herb mixture and apply salt and pepper to the overall body.

2. In a big skillet, prepare the olive oil over medium-high heat. When the oil is heated, place the chicken skin-side down in the skillet. Cook for about 5 minutes, or until the skin is crispy and golden. Cook the chicken on the other side in the same fashion. Remove the pan from the heat source and set it aside. Finish cooking the chicken in the oven, skin side up, for 15 minutes.

3. In the meantime, reheat the same pan over medium heat. Add 1 tablespoon of butter, melted. Include the cipollini onions and carrots after the butter has melted. Season to taste with salt and pepper. Cook for about 7 minutes, or until soft and golden in spots. Scrape some brown bits off the bottom of the pan with a wooden spoon before adding the chicken broth.

4. Throw the mushrooms and snap peas into the mix and allow to simmer for 5 minutes over low heat or until the vegetables are tender and the liquid has decreased by half. Season with pepper and salt, if desired.

5. Take the chicken out of the oven and place it on a serving platter. Place the vegetables, along with the chicken, on a serving platter. Using a spoon, drizzle the sauce over the chicken. Serve straight away.

Jicama Salad

Jicama salad is another meal you can enjoy during lunch. It is easy to prepare, taking only an hour of your time. You can serve 4 persons with the recipe detailed below.

Ingredients

1 large Jicama, sliced into thin strips

1 cup of red onion, finely sliced

½ red pepper, thinly sliced

2 large carrots, thinly sliced

1 tomato, thinly sliced

½ yellow pepper, thinly sliced

¼ cup of fresh lime juice

¼ cup of red wine vinegar

Pinch of cayenne

2 tbsp of olive oil

1 tsp of honey

Salt and freshly ground pepper

2 tbsp of chopped cilantro

Preparation

In a medium mixing dish, toss together the jicama, carrots, red onion, all peppers, and tomato. Season with salt and pepper to taste after whisking together the lime juice, sugar, butter, olive oil, and cayenne. Enable 30 minutes for the cilantro to infuse.

Mushroom Barley and Roasted Asparagus Salad

This diabetic meal takes 20 mins to prepare and 1 hour to cook. You may end up spending 2 hours before the food is ready. However, the diet is worth the effort. It is easy to prepare and serves 6 people. The nutritional value you will get include the following:

Calories: 258 calorie

Total fat: 14 grams

Saturated fat: 2 grams

Cholesterol: 0 milligram

Sodium: 689 milligrams

Carbohydrates: 29 grams

Dietary fiber: 8 grams

Protein: 7 grams

Sugar: 4 grams

Ingredients

2 sprigs of fresh thyme and 1 tbsp of minced leaves

¾ cup of pearl barley, rinsed

10 oz. of button mushrooms, trimmed and thinly sliced (4

cups)

2 lemons, zest peeled in large strips

3 stems of fresh parsley (flat-leaf) and 1/3 cup of chopped leaves

1/3 cup of freshly squeezed lemon juice

Freshly ground black pepper

2 tsp of Dijon mustard

2 tsp of kosher salt

½ medium shallot, minced

2 bunches of medium asparagus, trimmed woody stems (2 pounds)

Preparation

1. Fill a medium-sized bowl with barley. Just cover the

barley with water, around a few centimeters. Season generously with salt. Bay leaf, parsley leaves, lemon peel, and thyme sprigs are some of the ingredients to use. Using kitchen twine, connect them. Cook until the vegetables are soft. It takes about 30 minutes in most situations. Set aside the lemon and herbs.

2. In a big mixing cup, toss the mushrooms with 2 tablespoons lemon juice and 1/2 teaspoon salt. In a small cup, combine the remaining lemon juice, mustard, residual salt, and pepper to taste. Whisk in the olive oil in a steady line, starting with a few drops and working your way up to a creamy, somewhat thick vinaigrette. Toss in the shallots.

3. Mix barley, mushrooms, and dressing in chopped herbs. Allow the flavors to kick in by leaving the mixture at room temperature for 1 hour.

4. Preheat oven to 450 degrees Fahrenheit (230 degrees Celsius). In a shallow baking pan, spread the spears in a single layer, drizzle with olive oil, season with salt, and roll to thoroughly coat. Roast for about 10 minutes, or until the asparagus is gently browned and soft, shaking

the pan halfway through.

5. On a serving platter, spread the roasted asparagus. Serve with the barley salad on top.

Escarole and Beans Soup

This meal takes 12 minutes to prepare and 10 minutes to cook. It yields 6 servings.

Ingredients

2 tbsp of olive oil

2 garlic cloves, chopped

Salt

4 cups of chicken broth (low-salt)

1 pound of escarole, chopped

1 (1 oz.) piece of Parmesan

1 (15 oz.) can of cannellini beans, drained and rinsed

6 tsp of extra-virgin olive oil

Freshly ground black pepper

Preparation

1. Get a thick, big pot, heat 2 teaspoons olive oil over medium heat. Add the garlic and cook for about 15 seconds, or until fragrant. Attach the escarole and simmer for 2 minutes or until wilted. Season with a sprinkle of salt. Combine the chicken broth, beans, and Parmesan cheese in a large mixing bowl. Cover and cook for 5 minutes, or until the beans are well cooked. To taste, season with salt and pepper.

2. Ladle the broth into 6 pots with 1 teaspoon extra-virgin olive oil drizzled on each crusty toast, serve.

Halibut and Chickpea Salad

Halibut and chickpea salad provides you with a tasty

homemade meal experience even while at work. This delicious diet takes 20 minutes to prepare and 10 minutes to cook. Using the recipe below, you can serve between 4 to 6 persons.

<u>Ingredients</u>

1 (6 oz.) of halibut steak

¼ tsp of salt

2 tsp of extra-virgin olive oil

¼ tsp of freshly ground black pepper

1 cup of arugula, chopped

1 head endive, chopped

1 (15 oz.) can of chickpeas (garbanzo beans)

10 cherry tomatoes, halved

¼ cup of extra-virgin olive oil

1 fennel bulb, stalks removed, halved, and thinly sliced

2 tsp of honey

1 lemon, juiced

½ tsp of salt

1 tsp of ground cumin

½ tsp of freshly ground black pepper

<u>Preparation</u>

1. Heat a grill pan over medium-high heat for the halibut. Season the halibut on both sides with salt and pepper after brushing it with olive oil. 4 minutes per side on the grill until cooked through. Enable for a few minutes of resting time before cutting the fish into 1-inch cubes.

2. For the salad: In a wide bowl, mix the endive, arugula,

onions, chickpeas, and fennel. In a small bowl, blend the olive oil, lemon juice, honey, cumin, cinnamon, and pepper. Toss the salad with the olive oil mixture to blend it. Serve with the fish on top.

Lentil and Rice Salad

You can have this meal ready in 50 minutes. It takes 20 minutes to prepare and 30 minutes to cook. Servings range from 4 to 6 people.

Ingredients

1 carrot, peeled and finely diced

1 tbsp of extra-virgin olive oil, plus 3 tbsp

2 garlic cloves, minced

1 small onion, finely chopped

1 ¼ cups of dried green lentils

2 ½ cups of chicken broth, plus 2 cups

1 bay leaf

1 cup of long-grain white rice

½ cup of pitted kalamata olives, coarsely chopped

½ cup of chopped fresh Italian parsley leaves

2 tsp of finely grated lemon peel

1 tbsp of chopped fresh thyme leaves

2 tsp of finely grated lemon peel

Salt and freshly ground black pepper

Preparation

1. Get a big frying pan, heat 1 tablespoon oil. Sauté the carrot, onion, and garlic for about 5 minutes, or until the onion is translucent. Add the lentils and mix well. 2 12

cup broth, brought to a boil over high heat. Reduce the heat to a medium-low environment. Cover and cook for 15 minutes, or until the lentils are only tender. Drain thoroughly. Place the lentils in a large mixing bowl.

2. In a medium saucepan, bring the remaining 2 cups of broth and bay leaf to a boil over high heat. Return the broth to low heat and add the rice. Cover and cook over low heat, stirring occasionally, for about 20 minutes, or until the rice is soft and the liquid has been absorbed (do not stir the rice as it cooks).

3.Turn off the stove and remove the saucepan from the heat. With a large fork, fluff the rice. Place the lentils in a mixing bowl. Combine the olives, parsley, thyme, and lemon peel in a large mixing bowl.

4. Coat the rice mixture in the remaining 3 tablespoons of oil. Add salt and pepper to taste. Warm or room temperature are both acceptable serving options.

Manhattan Clam Chowder

Clams are simmered with bacon, vegetables, and potatoes

in a savory tomato broth in this Manhattan clam chowder. A hearty soup that's simple to prepare and works well as an appetizer or main course. This Manhattan clam chowder is great for seafood lovers. It's filled with clams, vegetables, and potatoes, and it's a healthier alternative to the creamy New England clam chowder. It takes 40 minutes to get ready – 15 minutes to prepare, 25 minutes to cook. It serves between 4 and 6 persons.

Ingredients

1 ½ tbsp olive oil

1 large Spanish onion, chopped

1 ½ celery stalks, chopped

7 cloves garlic, minced

Pinch crushed red pepper

¼ cup tomato paste

3 sprigs parsley

3 sprigs fresh thyme

1 bay leaf

1 large waxy-style potato (about ¾ pound), diced

5 cups of clam juice (five 8 oz. of bottled clam juice)

1 (1 oz.) can whole, peeled tomatoes (with liquid), roughly chopped

1 ½ cups minced clams, drained (about four 6 ½ oz. cans)

1 tbsp kosher salt or to taste

Freshly ground black pepper

2 tbsp of chopped parsley for garnish

Preparation

1. Place oil over medium heat and heat in a big pot. Ready and add to the pot the garlic, onion, celery, and crushed pepper. Stir it occasionally, cook the mixture for about 8 minutes. Add the tomato paste and cook, and remove for roughly 1 minute. Tie the bay leaf, fresh thyme, and parsley sprigs with a piece of kitchen twine before placing into the pot, alongside the potatoes.

2. Add clam juice to the contents and boil. Reduce heat and cook, covered, about 10 minutes until potatoes are tender. Tomatoes and palms in a combination. Take a low cooler and cover. Season to taste with pepper. Pour the meal into soup bowls and sprinkle with parsley. Serve straight away.

Pumpernickel, Ham, and Watercress Sandwich

Pumpernickel ham and watercress sandwich is one of the easiest delectable meals you can have during lunch. Above all, it is healthy, thanks to the rich nutrients it possesses. Preparing this meal takes only 5 minutes. It serves one.

Ingredients

1 tbsp of Dijon mustard

1 tsp of honey

3 oz. of lean ham

2 slices of pumpernickel bread

¼ cup of watercress, cleaned

Preparation

Whisk the Dijon and honey in a bowl to create a honey-mustard mixture. Spread this mixture on 1 bread slice and top with the ham and the watercress, alongside the remaining bread slice.

Minestrone Soup with Pasta, Beans, and Vegetables

The famous Italian minestrone comes packed with all the

nourishing goodness and flavors you can imagine. It is a hearty meal you would not want to miss. Readying this diabetic food takes 4 hours and 15 minutes – 15 minutes of preparation and 4 hours of cooking. It serves 4 people.

Ingredients

1 (28 oz.) can diced tomatoes

2 carrots, peeled and chopped

Salt and ground black pepper

2 cups of cooked ditalini pasta

1 medium zucchini, chopped

Basil sprigs, garnish, optional

1 celery stalk, chopped

1 cup of onion, chopped

1 teaspoon of dried thyme

½ tsp dried sage

2 bay leaves

4 tbsp of grated Parmesan or Romano cheese

3 cups of vegetable or chicken broth (reduced-sodium)

1 (15 oz.) can white (cannellini or navy) beans, drained

2 cups of coarsely chopped fresh or frozen spinach, defrosted

Preparation

1. Combine soup, tomatoes, celery, beans, carrots, thyme, onion, sage, baking leaves, and ½ teaspoon for each salt and black pepper in a slow cooker. Cover and simmer for 6 to 8 hours or 3 to 4 hours over high heat.

2. Add the ditalini, zucchini, and spinach 30 minutes

before the soup is done cooking. Cook for another 30 minutes, sealed. Remove the bay leaves and season with salt and black pepper to taste. Pour the broth into bowls and finish with parmesan cheese. If needed, garnish with basil.

Waldorf Salad

The Waldorf salad is one of the most basic and delicious salads available, as well as one of the healthiest. It is a nutrient-dense plate that can be mixed into any balanced diet. This dish, like all of our others, is lactose-free, gluten-free, and sugar-free. A Waldorf salad takes about 15 minutes to prepare and 10 minutes to cook for a total of 25 minutes. The recipe below serves 4 people. Here is the nutritional value it provides:

Calories: 221 calorie

Total fat: 11 grams

Saturated fat: 1 gram

Cholesterol: 3 milligrams

Sodium: 98 milligrams

Carbohydrates: 31 grams

Dietary fiber: 5 grams

Protein: 5 grams

Sugar: 22 grams

Ingredients

½ cup of walnuts halves

½ cup of non-fat yogurt

2 tbsp of light mayonnaise

2 tbsp of minced fresh flat-leaf parsley

1 tsp of honey

½ lemon, zest finely grated

Freshly ground black pepper

2 large crisp apples, such as Gala

2 ribs celery (with leaves), sliced into 1/2-inch-thick pieces (leaves chopped)

¼ cup of golden raisins

½ lemon, juiced

1 head Boston lettuce, trimmed, washed, and dried

<u>Preparation</u>

1. Preheat oven to 350 degrees Fahrenheit.

2. Toast the nuts for 8 to 10 minutes on a baking dish. Cool and cut the nuts up into little bits. Pour mayonnaise, honey, parsley, yogurt, and lemon zest into a large dish and whisk. Season the mixture with pepper.

3. Leave the skin on the apples and halve, heart, and cut them into 3/4-inch sections. Toss the apples, celery, and raisins in a large mixing bowl with the lemon juice and the dressing. If not serving right now, cover and chill.

4. Toss walnuts into the salad just before serving. Divide the lettuce leaves among four salad plates or arrange them on a large platter. Serve the salad on a plate of lettuce.

Raspberry Chicken Salad

Like some of the salads discussed in this section, the raspberry chicken salad is easy to prepare, setting you back by only 5 minutes. The recipe below caters to 4 persons.

Ingredients

¼ cup of raspberry preserves

2 tbsp of olive oil

1 tbsp of white wine vinegar

1 tsp of Dijon mustard

Salt and ground black pepper

2 tbsp of minced scallion

1 cup of fresh raspberries

4 cooked chicken breast halves, cut into 1-inch pieces

4 cups chopped Bibb lettuce

Nut bread

Cream cheese

Preparation

Whisk together the raspberry preserves, oil, Dijon mustard, vinegar, and salt and pepper in a medium-sized mixing bowl. Toss in the scallions and raspberries with the vinaigrette. Toss in the diced chicken with the vinaigrette to coat. On separate dishes, arrange the lettuce. Just before eating, spoon the chicken mixture onto the lettuce. If wanted, serve with cream cheese and nut bread.

Chicken Kebabs

Chicken kebab is has a straightforward recipe that you can change to meet your dieting needs, even as a diabetic. This classic barbecue staple can be stuffed into a pita or eaten over couscous salad. Replace the coriander with a moderate herb or leave it out altogether. The skewers are versatile in that they can be used to cook, roast, or barbecue your kebab. The preparation takes 30 minutes, while the cooking duration can be up to two hours. The recipe discussed below yields 6 servings. Kindly note that you will need skewers – 12 to 15 wooden pieces soaked in water for about 15 minutes.

Ingredients

1 cup of plain Greek yogurt

1tbsp of vegetable oil

½ tbsp of fresh lemon juice

2 cloves of garlic, smashed and chopped

1 tsp of dried oregano

Kosher salt and freshly ground black pepper

½ tsp of coriander

½ tsp of paprika

2 pounds of boneless, skinless chicken breast, diced into 1-inch cubes.

Preparation

1. In a medium dish, whisk together the yogurt, oil, lemon juice, oregano, coriander, paprika, garlic, ½ teaspoon salt, and ¼ teaspoon pepper. Toss in the chicken to coat it. Refrigerate for 2 to 4 hours after coating with plastic

wrap.

2. Preheat a barbecue pan or an outdoor grill to medium-high heat for preparation. Thread about 5 pieces of marinated chicken per skewer onto the soaked skewers, being careful not to overcrowd the chicken.

3. Grill the skewers for 4 minutes per side, or until the chicken is cooked through (an instant-read thermometer should read 165 degrees F). Serve right away.

Chicken (with Tabbouleh)

If chicken kebab does not appeal to you as a standalone, consider eating it alongside tabbouleh, a Lebanese salad. Tabbouleh is mostly consumed in the Arab world. The west, on the other hand, is warming up to this delicacy. Add some fried chicken to the mix, and you've got yourself a lunch worth enjoying. It takes 15 minutes to prepare, 35 minutes to cook, and an hour of inactivity. You can serve 6 to 8 people based on the recipe given below.

Ingredients

1 ½ cups of boiling water

1 cup of bulgur wheat

¼ cup of freshly squeezed lemon juice (2 lemons)

Olive oil

Kosher salt

1 whole (2 splits) chicken breast, bone-in, skin on

Freshly ground black pepper

1 cup of minced scallions, white and green parts (1 bunch)

1 cup of chopped fresh mint leaves (2 bunches)

1 cup of chopped fresh flat-leaf parsley (1 bunch)

1 hothouse cucumber, unpeeled, halved lengthwise, seeded, and medium-diced

2 cups of halved cherry tomatoes

Preparation

1. Preheat oven to 350 degrees Fahrenheit.

2. Pour the boiling water over the bulgur wheat in a heat-resistant cup. Combine the lemon juice, 1/4 cup olive oil, and 1 1/2 teaspoons salt in a mixing bowl. Stir it up a little. Cover the bowl with plastic wrap and set it aside for 1 hour to allow the bulgur to come to room temperature.

3. Rub the chicken breast with olive oil and place it on a baking sheet. Season generously with salt and pepper. Roast for 35–40 minutes, or until the chicken is just cooked through. Enable to cool completely.

4. Remove the meat from the bones and throw away the flesh. Toss the tabbouleh with the chicken, which has been cut into medium dice. 2 teaspoons garlic, 1 teaspoon pepper, scallions, mint, parsley, cucumber, onions, and 2 teaspoons salt Season with salt and pepper to taste, then serve right away or cover and chill. As it cools down, the tastes will improve.

Slow-Roasted Salmon with Cucumber Dill Salad

If you want something outside the traditional chicken salad, this meal is for you. What more can be better than a raspberry chicken salad? Of course, a slow-roasted salmon with cucumber dill salad. It takes 20 minutes to prepare the ingredients, another 20 minutes to cook, and also 1 hour of inactivity. It comes with its nutritional values as well:

Calories: 369 calorie

Total fat: 23 grams

Saturated fat: 5 grams

Cholesterol: 95 milligrams

Sodium: 797 milligrams

Carbohydrates: 7 grams

Dietary fiber: 1 gram

Protein: 39 grams

Sugar: 4 grams

Ingredients

1 English (seedless) cucumber (about 1 pound)

1 tbs kosher salt

1 cup of low-fat plain yogurt

2 tsp of roughly chopped fresh dill (2 fronds), with additional fronds for garnish

½ tsp of finely grated orange zest

Pinch sugar

Freshly ground black pepper

Pinch cayenne pepper

1 ½ pound of center-cut salmon, skinned

Kosher salt (for the fish)

¼ tsp of ground turmeric

<u>Preparation</u>

1. To make the salad, cut the cucumber in half lengthwise and extract the seeds but not the flesh. In a colander, thinly slice the cucumbers and combine them with the salt. Drain for about an hour in the sink. In the meantime, wash the yogurt in a coffee filter-lined strainer over a bucket for about an hour.

2. Using cool, flowing water, rinse the cucumbers. To remove as much liquid as possible from the cucumbers, press down on them and pat them dry. Toss cucumbers with dill, soaked yogurt, cayenne, sugar, orange zest, and pepper to taste.

3. Preheat oven to 275 degrees Fahrenheit.

4. To make 4 equivalent squares of salmon, cut the salmon lengthwise and then crosswise. Sprinkle a pinch of turmeric all over the salmon and rub it in gently to coat uniformly. Season the salmon with salt and pepper and put it in an oven-safe nonstick pan that has been lightly oiled. Roast the salmon for about 20 minutes, rotating the bits gently with a spatula after about 10 minutes, until just cooked through. (When done, slow-roasted salmon will be light orange in color and luscious in the center.) To eat, split the cucumbers among four dishes, then top with the salmon and dill fronds.

Greek Salad with Oregano Marinated Chicken

Indeed, Greek salad has only gotten a whole lot better. What secret does this mouth-watering dish hold? The super moist, perfectly crispy chicken thighs flavored with oregano, basil, thyme, paprika, and garlic powder in a dry spice rub? It is so much more than that. You do not need to marinate for hours. Simply season the chicken and put it directly on the grill. It is as simple as it gets. Kindly note that it takes 1 hour, 15 minutes to be ready – 30 minutes for preparation, 30 minutes for inactivity, and 15 minutes for cooking. The recipe for this meal serves between 4 to 6 individuals. Coupled with that is the nutritional value analysis, highlighted below:

Calories: 544 calorie

Total fat: 34 grams

Saturated fat: 6 grams

Cholesterol: 135 milligrams

Sodium: 1008 milligrams

Carbohydrates: 12 grams

Dietary fiber: 3 grams

Protein: 46 grams

Sugar: 5 grams

Ingredients

For the chicken:

1 lemon, juiced

2 tbsp of extra-virgin olive oil

1 tsp of dried oregano

Salt (two pinches)

10 grinds of black pepper

4 (6 to 7 oz.) boneless skinless chicken breasts

For the dressing:

¼ cup of extra-virgin olive oil

2 tbsp of red wine vinegar

1 lemon, juiced

2 cloves of garlic (smashed)

1 tsp of oregano

3 pinches of salt

10 to 15 grinds of black pepper

For the salad:

1 English cucumber, peeled, cut in ½ lengthwise and ½-inch chunks

2 to 3 hearts of romaine lettuce

3 vine-ripened tomatoes (3/4 pound), cored and cut into ½-inch chunks

½ red onion, very thinly sliced

½ cup of pitted kalamata olives, coarsely chopped

¼ cup of crumbled feta cheese

Preparation

1. To marinate the chicken, combine the lemon juice, olive oil, oregano, salt, and pepper in a non-reactive dish and whisk to combine. Rub all sides of the chicken breasts in the paste. Refrigerate for at least 30 minutes and up to 4 hours after wrapping the dish with plastic wrap.

2. To make the dressing: Combine all the ingredients in a resealable container and shake vigorously. Refrigerate until ready to eat, and then hold to room temperature before tossing lettuce.

3. Cut the dark tips and bitter white bottoms off the romaine leaves before assembling the salad. Cut the lettuce into 1-inch strips and place in a bowl large enough to comfortably hold all of the salad ingredients. Top with cucumbers, tomatoes, red onion, olives, and feta. You can make the salad ahead of time, up to a few hours. Refrigerate it for 30 minutes after covering it with a moist paper towel.

4. Heat a nonstick skillet or grill pan over high heat to prepare the chicken. Cook, rotating once until the chicken

breasts are well browned and cooked through, around 4 to 5 minutes per side. Before chopping the chicken into thin slices, let it rest for a few minutes on a cutting board.

5. Shake the dressing properly before pouring it into a small serving dish, straining out the garlic with the lid. Toss the salad and serve.

Open Face Lean Roast Beef Sandwich

This unique meal comes with a straightforward preparatory process. It takes 20 minutes to prepare the ingredient and 28 minutes to cook it. Serving is pegged at 4 people for the recipe below.

Ingredients

1 ½ pound of red-skinned potatoes, pierced with a fork

4 tbsp of unsalted butter

¾ to 1 cup of milk

½ medium onion, sliced

Kosher salt and freshly ground pepper

3 tbsp of all-purpose flour

2 tsp of Worcestershire sauce

2 ½ cups of chicken broth (low-sodium)

4 thick slices of sourdough bread

1 tbsp of prepared horseradish

3 tbsp of Dijon mustard

½ bunch of watercress, woody stems removed

¼ cup of chopped fresh parsley

¾ pound of sliced roast beef

Preparation

1. Microwave the potatoes on high for 20 minutes or until tender. Mash the potatoes with 2 tablespoons butter in a mixing bowl using a fork. Mash in the milk, seasoning with salt and pepper. Preheat the oven to broil.

2. In the meantime, in a pan over high pressure, melt the remaining 2 teaspoons butter. Cook, stirring sometimes, until the onion is tender, around 4 minutes. Cook, stirring continuously until the flour is finely browned. Whisk in the chicken broth in small increments until smooth. Stir in the Worcestershire sauce and cook for 3 minutes, or until thickened.

3. Broil for 1 minute to toast the bread. Place each toast on a plate and spread with mustard and horseradish. Pour some gravy over the toast, then pile the roast beef, more gravy, watercress, and parsley on top. Using salt and pepper, season to taste. Potatoes can be eaten with sandwiches.

Spicy Bean Soup

There are bean soups, and then there is the spicy bean soup, a special delicacy that comes with an extra kick. It boasts the presence of seasonal vegetables and chili pepper. There may be variations as some individuals prefer the use of chili powder. Nevertheless, the aroma and taste of this soup will leave you craving for more. It takes 1 hour, 5 minutes to have this meal fully ready – 20 minutes goes into preparing the meal, while 45 minutes goes into cooking it. The recipe below yields 10 servings.

Ingredients

3 tbsp of olive oil

2 onions, chopped

2 celery stalks, cut into ½-inch pieces

1 carrot, peeled and cut into ½-inch pieces

1 red bell pepper, cut into ½-inch pieces

6 cloves of garlic, finely chopped

½ cup of chili powder

1 tbsp of ground coriander

1 tbsp of ground cumin

2 tsp of dried oregano

1 tsp of dried crushed red pepper, optional

2 (14 ½ oz.) cans diced tomatoes with juices

1 (11 ½ oz.) can tomato juice

1 (6 oz.) can tomato paste

1 (3-inch) piece Parmesan cheese rind, optional

2 tsp of salt, plus more to taste

8 cups vegetable or chicken broth

2 (15 ½ oz.) cans garbanzo beans, drained and rinsed

2 (15 oz.) cans cannellini beans, drained and rinsed

½ cup of dried green lentils

3 cups of broccoli florets

2 zucchini, cut crosswise into ½-inch thick rounds

2 yellow crookneck squash, cut crosswise into ½-inch thick rounds

½ cup of freshly shredded Parmesan

¼ cup of thinly sliced fresh basil leaves

Preparation

1. Get a heavy, big stockpot. Pour oil into it and heat over medium-high heat. Place the carrot, celery, garlic, bell pepper, and onion into the pot. Saute for 15 minutes or until the onions become brown. Add coriander, chili powder, oregano, cumin, and crushed red pepper into the mix.

2. Cook for 2 minutes. Include tomato paste, tomato juice,

cheese rind, and 2 teaspoons of salt. Add lentils, cannellini beans, garbanzo beans, and broth. Do the same for the yellow squash, zucchini, and broccoli and stir.

3. Allow the food content to simmer over high heat before decreasing the heat to medium. Leave the pot uncovered and stir occasionally as the food simmers until the mixture becomes thick and lentils are tender around 20 minutes.

4. Add more salt (if required) to give the stew an improved taste. Pour the stew into clean bowls and sprinkle with basil and shredded cheese. Serve immediately.

Poached Salmon with Lemon Mint Tzatziki

This meal comes with several health benefits and is ideal for individuals battling diabetes. It takes 3 hours, 18 minutes to have it fully ready – 10 minutes of preparation, 3 hours of inactivity, and 8 minutes of cooking. It serves 6 individuals. The list below contains information on its nutritional value.

Calories: 307 calorie

Total fat: 17 grams

Saturated fat: 3 grams

Carbohydrates: 4 grams

Protein: 32 grams

Ingredients

2 cups of dry white wine

2 cups of water

2 bay leaves

2 sprigs flat-leaf parsley

2 lemons, unpeeled, sliced

1 (2-pound) salmon fillet with skin

1 scallion, top only, thinly sliced

1 cup of Lemon Mint Tzatziki

For lemon-mint tzatziki:

1 cup of non-fat yogurt

1 English cucumber

1 tsp of olive oil

2 tsp of lemon juice

½ tsp of minced garlic

¼ tsp of lemon zest

1 tsp of finely chopped mint leaves

Salt and pepper

Preparation

1. Combine the bay leaves, parsley, wine, water, and sliced lemons in a big, deep skillet and bring to a simmer.

2. Place the salmon skin-side down in the pan. To protect the salmon, add more water if possible. Cover the pan and simmer over low heat for 8 minutes or until the fish is just cooked through.

3. Transfer the fish to a pan, cover it, and chill it for at least 3 hours in the refrigerator.

4. Remove the skin from the fillet and scrape away some brown skin before eating. Place the fish on a serving plate and top with the remaining lemon slices and scallion. Serve with Tzatziki with Lemon-Mint.

For the Lemon Mint Tzatziki:

Yield: 1 cup

1. Place a paper towel in a strainer and align properly. Put the strainer over a bowl. Pour the yogurt into the strainer and refrigerate to drain and thicken for 3 hours.

2. Remove the seeds from the cucumber and grate coarsely. Drain the contents. Pour the thickened yogurt and olive oil into a medium-sized bowl and stir. Add zest, garlic, lemon juice, mint, and cucumber, and stir. Include pepper and salt to taste. Serve immediately.

Beet and Mandarin Orange Salad with Mint

Beet and Mandarin orange salad with mint is one of the diabetic meals that you can prepare in under 5 minutes. It serves 4 people. You can enjoy this meal while on the go as preparation is straightforward.

Ingredients

1 can of mandarin oranges, drain, reserving 2 tbsp of juice

2 tbsp of olive oil

2 tbsp of red wine vinegar

1 can of sliced beets, drained

1 sprig mint, leaves torn

Preparation

Extract 2 tablespoons of juice from the can of mandarin oranges while draining. Mix the juice with red wine vinegar and olive oil in a mixing bowl. Toss oranges and beets and top with mint.

Chicken and Pasta Soup

Are you looking for a meal that brightens your world even on a gloomy day? Perhaps, you want that meal that fills your home with a delightful, classic soup aroma. Chicken and pasta soup is your go-to meal anytime, any day, and anywhere. The preparation step is straightforward, making it easy for anyone to cook. However, you may spend more time preparing the chicken and veggies. Many households enjoy this lip-smacking, flavored meal, which packs a punch of several nutrients.

Include Shallots (flavor enhancers) in your meal to give it a traditional French-like taste. There are a lot of fresh herbs, in truth, a double layer of herbs! As the soup simmers, fresh rosemary and thyme are added, and a final portion is stirred in. The bay leaves bring a delicate yet tasty layer of flavor to the chicken broth. With a few easy moves, you can get a delicious taste. Both youngsters and adults enjoy this meal, even seeking second servings. You can have this meal ready in 30 minutes – 10 minutes to prepare, 20 minutes to cook. For 9 cups, you can get 4 to 6 servings.

Ingredients

1 cup of orzo or favorite-shaped little pasta

1 tbsp of extra-virgin olive oil

½ medium onion, diced

1 garlic clove, minced

1 medium carrot, shredded

1 rib celery, peeled and minced

½ tsp of kosher salt

3 cups of cooked chicken

1 bay leaf

1 sprig of fresh thyme

5 cups of chicken broth, low-sodium canned or homemade

Preparation

Pour cold water into a big-sized pot, salt generously, and boil over high heat. Place the pasta into the pot and boil, stirring at intervals for 8 minutes or until tender. Drain the contents.

Add oil to a large frying pan and leave it under medium heat. Pour carrot, onion, celery, garlic, and salt into the saucepan. Cook the mixture for 8 minutes or until tender. Add the broth, chicken, thyme, and bay leaf. Simmer for 10 minutes, covered.

Before serving, add the pasta to the soup. Serve directly in warm cups. Keep any leftovers (if any) in the refrigerator for later consumption.

Chickpea and Spinach Salad with Cumin Dressing and Yogurt Sauce

Who says that you cannot enjoy a sumptuous and wholesome salad with the richness of chickpea, spinach, cumin, and mint. Underneath the plethora of soothing flavors, you can feel a tang of lime, giving your meal an irresistible taste. Chickpea and spinach with cumin dressing and yogurt sauce come with an easy-to-make process. The difficulty level for this meal is easy. You can prepare and serve it in under 20 minutes. It caters to 8 persons. Here is the nutritional value analysis per serving:

Calories: 163 calorie

Total fat: 8.5 grams

Saturated fat: 0.9 grams

Cholesterol: 0 milligrams

Sodium: 147 milligrams

Carbohydrates: 18 grams

Dietary fiber: 5 grams

Protein: 5.4 grams

<u>Ingredients</u>

2 (15 oz.) cans chickpeas, drained and rinsed

¼ cup of flat-leaf parsley (chopped)

½ cup of red onion (chopped)

¼ cup of olive oil

3 tbsp of lemon juice

½ tsp of lemon zest

1 ½ tsp of ground cumin

4 cups of baby spinach leaves

1/8 tsp of cayenne pepper

Salt and pepper

Yogurt with orange essence (recipe stated below) (optional)

2 tbsp of fresh mint leaves (coarsely chopped) (optional)

Recipe for yogurt with orange essence:

¼ tsp of orange zest

1/3 cup of plain yogurt (low-fat)

½ tsp of honey

2 tbsp of orange juice

Preparation

Combine the chickpeas, parsley, and onion in a medium mixing dish. Whisk together the olive oil, lemon juice, zest, cumin, cayenne pepper, salt, and pepper in a shallow cup. Toss the chickpea mixture with the dressing to blend. Over a bed of spinach leaves, serve the chickpea salad. Finish with a dollop of yogurt sauce and a sprinkle of mint.

Yogurt with Orange Essence:

Yield: About ½ cup

Combine the yogurt, orange zest, orange juice, and honey in a shallow mixing bowl.

These are some of the meals you can enjoy for lunch. Most of them are included in the 30-day plan shared with you previously. Discuss your dietary plan with your dietician to get the best result.

Diabetes Meal Recipes for Dinner

If you are living with diabetes, eating a balanced diet doesn't have to mean giving up your favorite food. The secret to maintaining a healthy lifestyle is to consume in moderation and to maintain a combination of proteins, carbohydrates, and fats, with a priority on fiber. You can enjoy scrumptious meals, like salmon, steak, garden salad, steamed asparagus, sweet potato, white meat, and even burgers. The meals discussed in this section have low calories and are delightful to try out during dinners. They have a low glycemic index as well.

The dinner dietary recipes in this section are light and will keep you refreshed all through the night, enriching your body with the right nutrients. When eating these meals, remember that portion size is essential. It gives you control over what you take and how you take it. The "plate method" will make it easy for you to keep track of your portion size. It is so effective that several notable establishments, including the American Diabetes Association, approve of it. It is perfect for putting together dinner menus and meal plans. Here are some pointers to get you started:

Make a line down the center of your plate with an imaginary line.

One half can be split into two more parts, resulting in a three-part segmentation.

Add non-starchy vegetables to the biggest section. These veggies include green beans, mushrooms, lettuce, broccoli, salsa, and many more.

Fill any of the smaller sections (equivalent to a ¼th of the plate) with proteins, including salmon, tofu, shrimp, lean turkey, and skinless chicken. Some meals provide both protein and starch, an example being legumes. You can place such food in any of the smaller sections.

Fill the remaining section of the plate with food, like whole-grain bread, sweet potatoes, beans, corn, and quinoa. Each of them has its group, ranging from grains to starchy vegetables to legumes.

Add a diary or fruit serving to your diet.

You can conveniently monitor your nutrient intake by following the above guidelines. Dinners for diabetics don't have to be devoid of dessert or treats. However, the trick lies in avoiding carbohydrate-rich foods like pasta or bread during the main course of the meal. The "saved" carbs can be used on a small dessert. Also, check your blood sugar two hours after each diet. Here are some meals you can enjoy as dinners.

Grilled Ratatouille

What comes to mind when you think of the word "Ratatouille"? The notable vegetable delicacy of Italian origin? This delectable dish is jam-packed with vitamins and minerals from ingredients like tomatoes, brinjal, and zucchini. Ratatouille is a staple meal for all, and it's usually eaten with rice or pasta. Rice, on the other hand, is on the upper end of the glycemic index (GI) scale. It frequently causes blood sugar levels to increase, rendering it unsuitable for diabetics. The cooking level for this meal is "intermediate." It takes 33 minutes to have your food ready – 25 minutes for preparation and 8 minutes for cooking. Servings range from 4 to 6.

Ingredients

Salt

1-pint cherry tomatoes

Freshly ground pepper

2 red onions (quartered)

4 garlic cloves (finely chopped)

¼ cup of flat-leaf parsley leaves

½ cup of olive oil and 2 extra tbsp

2 Japanese eggplant (halved lengthwise)

2 zucchini (cut into quarters lengthwise)

2 yellow squash (cut into quarters lengthwise)

2 tbsp of fresh oregano leaves (finely chopped)

2 red bell peppers (stemmed, seeded, and quartered)

2 yellow bell peppers (stemmed, seeded, and quartered)

Preparation

1. Preheat the grill to medium-high temperature.

2. Put the tomatoes and vegetables in a bowl. Pour ½ cup of olive oil into the mixture to coat. Add pepper and salt to taste. Cook the vegetables on the grill for 5 to 6 minutes, turning halfway into the cooking time. Take the tomatoes off the grill, leaving the rest covered to cook for 2 minutes or until almost cooked.

3. Coarsely slice the vegetables on a cutting board (leave tomatoes whole). In a large mixing cup, blend the diced vegetables and tomatoes, oregano, olive oil, 2 tablespoons, garlic, and parsley. Add salt and pepper to taste. Allow cooling before serving.

Grilled Tuna Steaks with Black Sesame Seeds

Tuna has several health advantages, including cardiovascular benefits. This fish is high in niacin (vitamin B3) and omega-3 fatty acids, making it a good choice for diabetics. High cholesterol isn't something to be concerned about. Niacin is nearly 16 milligrams per 3-ounce serving of fresh yellowfin tuna. Similarly, 11 milligrams of niacin are found in the same amount of canned tuna.

A 3-ounce serving of canned light water-packed tuna (drained) contains about 73 calories and 0.8 grams of fat, while the same quantity of tuna canned in oil (drained) contains 168 calories and 7 grams of fat. Grilled tuna steaks are an excellent alternative to a variety of tuna options (including water-packed tuna with mashed avocado). This high-fiber low-cholesterol meal takes 20 minutes to make – 10 minutes for preparing and 10 minutes for cooking. It also supports four individuals.

Ingredients

Cooking spray

4 (5 oz.) tuna steaks

¼ cup of honey mustard

Black pepper (salt and coarsely ground)

2 tbsp of black sesame seeds or regular variant

Preparation

Preheat a medium-high stovetop grill pan, skillet, or griddle sprayed with cooking spray. Season the tuna steaks with salt and black pepper to taste. Apply honey mustard and sesame seeds on both sides of the steaks and mix properly. Grill for 3 to 4 minutes on either side until medium – fork tender.

Angel Food Cake with Mango Sauce

If you are tired of plain and boring dairy-free desserts, angel food cake with mango soup will take your dieting to a whole new level. This sweet, tender, and spongy meal will have you craving for more as each ingredient comes alive in your mouth. It s healthy for individuals with diabetes, especially the type 2 condition. However, consume this meal in moderation. You can always enjoy this diet on the go, as it is easy to prepare. Have your colorful and lip-smacking delicacy ready in 10 minutes. Angel food cake with mango sauce serves 8 people based on the recipe shared below. The nutritional value for each daily serving is stated below.

Calories: 107 calorie

Carbohydrates: 25 grams

Dietary fiber: 1 gram

Protein: 2 grams

Ingredients

1 tbsp of sugar

2 tbsp of fresh lime juice

¼ cup of fresh mint leaves

1 (13 oz.) store-bought angel food cake

2 mangoes, peeled and cut into chunks (3 cups)

2 tsp of orange liqueur (recommended: Cointreau), optional

Preparation

Puree 1 of the mangoes with the lime juice, Cointreau, and sugar in a blender or food processor until smooth. The remaining mango should be sliced. Share the cake into halves, drizzle 1 tablespoon of mango sauce over each slice, then finish with diced mango. Serve with mint leaves as a garnish.

Grilled Chicken with Tomato-Cucumber Salad

What better to enjoy your grilled chicken than pairing it with tomato-cucumber salad. Is cucumber an ideal squash for diabetics? Of course, it is low in calories and high in nutrients. Cucumber is a source of protein, vitamin B, vitamin C, vitamin K, potassium, magnesium, phosphorus, and biotin. It has a GI number of 15, beating apple (38), grapefruit (25), watermelon (72), and bananas (52). Cucumber lowers blood sugar levels. Tomatoes have a GI number that is lower than that of cucumber, making it also a healthy combination. Process these food products into a salad and pair it with your grilled chicken, and you will have a combo pack of delightful, nourishing diet to make your dinner worth enjoying. You can ready your meal in 23 minutes – 15 minutes for preparation and 8 minutes for cooking. It yields 4 servings. Here is the nutritional value for this recipe per serving:

Calories: 203 calorie

Total fat: 5 grams

Saturated fat: 1 gram

Cholesterol: 66 milligrams

Sodium: 745 milligrams

Carbohydrates: 10 grams

Dietary fiber: 2 grams

Protein: 29 grams

Sugar: 6 grams

Ingredients

Salad:

1 clove of garlic

1 tbsp of chopped fresh dill

Freshly ground black pepper

1 tsp of extra-virgin olive oil

¼ lemon, juiced (about 1 tbsp)

1 tsp of kosher salt, plus more to taste

1 cup of pear tomatoes, sliced in rounds

3 pepperoncini peppers, stemmed and minced

1 Kirby cucumber, unpeeled, quartered lengthwise, and sliced

Grilled Chicken:

4 (4 oz.) chicken paillards (scaloppini)

Olive oil spray

Freshly ground black pepper

Preparation

Prepare a smashed mixture of garlic clove and salt (1 tsp). Mash it to form a gritty paste, a garlic crusher, or the grind-line of a knife. Mix the garlic paste with lemon juice and olive oil in a mixing dish. Toss pepperoncini, cucumber, dill, and onions. Pour a couple of black pepper in the mixture to taste. Toss and then set aside.

Preheat a nonstick skillet or grill pan to medium-high. Spray the chicken paillards gently with olive oil. Add salt and black pepper to season. Prepare the paillards in batches to prevent overcrowding when grilling. Grill the paillard, flipping once about 2 minutes on each side until cooked. Serve the chicken with tomato-cucumber salad topping.

Baked Mahi Mahi with Wine and Herbs

Mahi Mahi is one meal that you cannot get tired of regardless of how often you consume it. Every diet seems to reintroduce you to this amazing food, even when you try different white fish or white wines. In the end, you will always look forward to making a new plate. Even when you are not using parsley or bay leaf, you still end up with a meal with rich nutrients and flavor. Making a plate of this sumptuous only takes about 45 minutes – 20 minutes to prepare and 25 minutes to cook. For the recipe shared below, baked Mahi Mahi comes with 4 servings.

Ingredients

¾ cup dry vermouth

4 sprigs of fresh thyme

8 sprigs of fresh parsley

8 cloves garlic, smashed

2 bay leaves, preferably fresh

4 tbsp of extra-virgin olive oil

4 (6 oz.) skinless Mahi-Mahi fillets

2 tsp of freshly squeezed lemon juice

Kosher salt and freshly ground black pepper

12 cherry or pear red and yellow tomatoes for garnish

Preparation

1. Preheat the oven to 450 degrees Fahrenheit.

2. Using a medium baking dish or grating dish, arrange 4 parsley sprigs, thyme, and bay leaves in a bed of herbs. Sprinkle the top with garlic. Add salt and pepper to the fish sides to season.

3. Put the fish on the herbs. Include vermouth in the mix, followed by a drizzle of oil (2 tbsp) over the fish. Wrap the

rim of the dish loosely, using foil. Bake the fish for 15 to 20 minutes until opaque. The exact time depends on the size of the fillets.

4. Set the fish aside and gently drain the pan juices into a shallow saucepan. Save the garlic cloves and 4 thyme sprigs for later. Bring the sauce to a boil over high heat and steam for 5 minutes, or until it has reduced by half. In a separate dish, mix the remaining 2 teaspoons of olive oil and the lemon juice. Salt and pepper to taste. Keep separately.

5. Distribute the fish among four serving dishes. Garnish it with the 4 remaining parsley sprigs, tomatoes, and reserved garlic and thyme, before pouring the sauce over the cod.

Thai Style Shrimp Stir-Fry with Tomatoes and Basil

Thai-style shrimp stir-fry with tomatoes and basil may have an extensive list of ingredients, and you may do a lot of chopping. But the meal is worth the effort. Include the fresh basil and mint to give it that tingly taste and aroma.

The chili flakes and jalapeno in the food give you that spicy kick, which is balanced by lemon juice. The diabetic-friendly meal goes easy on your waistline. You save calories while enjoying the Thai shrimp stir-fry, which takes 30 minutes to make. 20 minutes go into preparing the meal, while 10 minutes go into cooking it. It yields 4 servings. Below is the nutritional value you get per serving:

Calories: 226 calorie

Total fat: 12 grams

Saturated fat: 2 grams

Cholesterol: 143 milligrams

Sodium: 1336 milligrams

Carbohydrates: 13 grams

Dietary fiber: 2 grams

Protein: 18 grams

Sugar: 7 grams

Ingredients

2 tbsp of soy sauce

1 tbsp of water

4 tsp of light brown sugar

2 tsp of Southeast Asian fish sauce

3 tbsp of peanut oil

3 garlic cloves, chopped

½ to 1 tsp of red chile flakes

2 cups of cherry tomatoes, halved

¼ cup of torn fresh mint leaves

¾ cup of torn fresh basil leaves

½ medium red onion, cut in 1-inch dice

1 tbsp of grated, peeled, fresh ginger

1 jalapeno chile, thinly sliced into rounds

2 tbsp of freshly squeezed lime juice

1 medium yellow pepper, seeded, cut in 1-inch dice

1 pound of large shrimp, peeled and deveined

Preparation

1. Mix water, sugar, fish sauce, and soy sauce in a small bowl and place aside. Pour oil into a large non-stick pan and heat over medium-high heat. Add ginger, chile flakes, and garlic to the oil and fry for 30 seconds, until aromatic. Pour in the shrimp and stir-fry for 2 minutes until pink but translucent in the middle. Move the shrimp to a medium bowl.

2. Add chile, pepper, and onion to the pan and stir-fry for 2 minutes until lightly brown. Transfer the shrimp to the pan. Add soy sauce mixture. Boil and stir-fry the mixture for 1 minute or until the sauce glazes the shrimp. Pour the tomatoes and stir for 15 seconds until it is coated with sauce. Take the skillet pan off the heat. Add mint, basil, and lime juice and stir. Serve in a dish.

Garlic-Lime Chicken with Olives

Enjoy the savory taste of crispy chicken garnished with lime, garlic, and olives. The low-fat, lean diet is healthy and full of flavors that will have you smacking your lips. Garlic-lime chicken with olives takes 40 minutes to fully prepare – 10 minutes for preparation and 30 minutes for cooking. Here is the nutritional information for the recipe:

Calories: 436 calorie

Total fat: 6 grams

Cholesterol: 197 milligrams

Sodium: 694 milligrams

Carbohydrates: 11 grams

Dietary fiber: 2 grams

Protein: 80 grams

Sugar: 5 grams

Ingredients

Nonstick cooking spray

1 cup of diced onion

2 to 3 garlic cloves (minced)

2 tbsp of fresh lime juice

1 tbsp of molasses

½ tsp of salt

1 tsp of dried oregano

1 ½ tsp of ground cumin

2 tsp of Worcestershire sauce

½ tsp of ground black pepper

½ cup of pitted and sliced Greek olives, such as kalamata

3 pounds of boneless skinless chicken breast halves (This amount of chicken is enough for three chicken-based meals. Use 1 pound if you are going to use it for this dinner alone.)

Preparation

1. Preheat the oven to 400 degrees Fahrenheit.

2. Apply cooking spray to a big roasting pan.

3. Add chicken, lime juice, garlic, onion, cumin, molasses, Worcestershire sauce, oregano, black pepper, and salt in a

large mixing bowl.

4. Prepare a pan. Move the chicken and remaining marinade (if any) to it. Place olives on top of and around the chicken in the pan. Roast for 30 to 3 minutes, or until chicken is thoroughly baked. For dinner, serve 1/3 of the chicken and refrigerate the rest for future meals.

Snapper with Roasted Grape Tomatoes, Garlic, and Basil

Your dinner does not have to necessarily be shrimp- or chicken-based. You can also throw the easy-to-make snapper meal garnished with roasted grape tomatoes, garlic, and basil. Complement the tomatoes with kosher salt, red pepper flakes, and balsamic vinegar to give your diet that wholesome goodness and nutrition your body needs. The recipe is easy to follow, and you will have your meal ready in 30 minutes – 10 minutes to prepare and 20 minutes to cook. It serves 4 people. Check out the nutritional value per serving below:

Calories: 254 calories

Total fat: 10 grams

Saturated fat: 2 grams

Carbohydrates: 5 grams

Dietary fiber: 1 gram

Protein: 36 grams

Ingredients

2 cups of grape tomatoes, halved

2 garlic cloves, sliced

Pinch red pepper flakes

½ cup of fresh basil leaves, torn

2 tbsp of extra-virgin olive oil

4 (6 oz.) snapper fillets, with skin

1 tsp of balsamic vinegar

Freshly ground black pepper

Kosher salt

Preparation

1. Preheat the oven to 350 degrees Fahrenheit with a rack in the middle.

2. Place the tomatoes on a baking sheet, adding vinegar, pepper flakes, garlic, salt, and 1 tablespoon of olive oil to taste. Roast for 15 minutes until tomatoes get juicy. Move the tomatoes into a casserole dish and spice with basil.

3. Get the snapper fillets (thoroughly dry) and gently slash a cross-hatch pattern on the fish skin using a sharp knife. Place the fish straight in the pan. Brush the remaining olive oil on the fish's rounded flesh edge, adding salt and pepper to taste.

4. Heat a large non-stick skillet over medium-high.

Position the fish in the oil, seasoned side down, and cook for 3 minutes until opaque on its edges and golden at the bottom. Season the skin side of the fish with a pinch of salt. Turn the fish over to its other side. Switch off the stove and let the snapper cook in the remaining heat of the pan for another minute or until it's firm but still juicy.

5. Divide the fish between four bowls. Serve with the tomatoes on top.

Chopped Nicoise Salad

Nicoise salad is one of the all-time favorites in several households. The preparation process for this diabetic-friendly meal can be intricate. Substantial time goes into cooking the green beans, potatoes, and eggs. However, you spend about 15 minutes preparing your ingredients and an additional 21 minutes cooking the meal. The recipe below serves 4 people (2-cup). Here is the nutritional value for the meal:

Calories: 267 calorie

Total fat: 10 grams

Saturated fat: 1.5 grams

Carbohydrates: 21 grams

Dietary fiber: 6 grams

Protein: 25 grams

Ingredients

1 quart of water

¼ tsp of salt

8 oz. of green beans

2 large eggs

3 quarts of water

2 tsp honey

2 Tbsp olive oil

½ lemon (juiced)

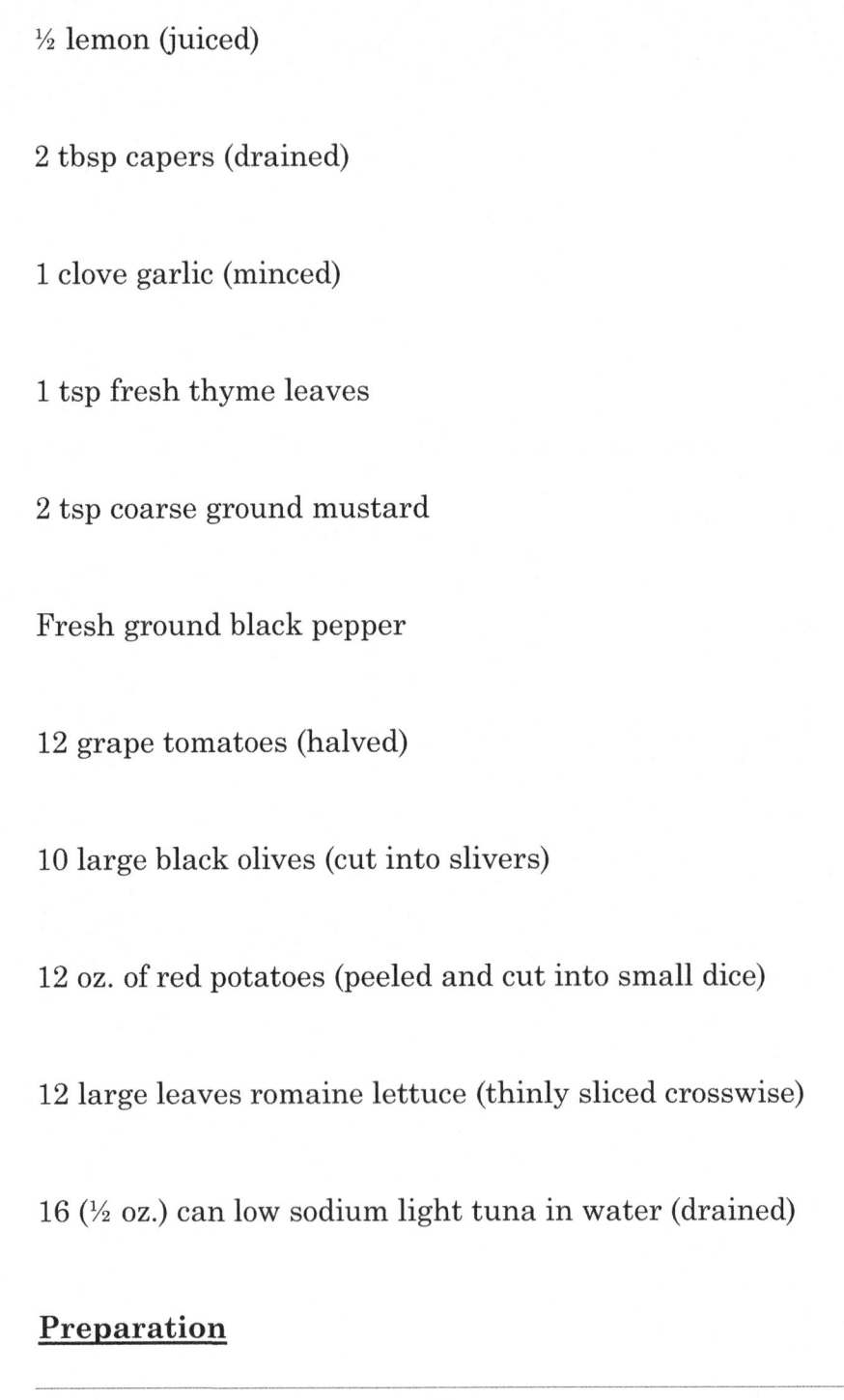

2 tbsp capers (drained)

1 clove garlic (minced)

1 tsp fresh thyme leaves

2 tsp coarse ground mustard

Fresh ground black pepper

12 grape tomatoes (halved)

10 large black olives (cut into slivers)

12 oz. of red potatoes (peeled and cut into small dice)

12 large leaves romaine lettuce (thinly sliced crosswise)

16 (½ oz.) can low sodium light tuna in water (drained)

Preparation

1. Bring 1 quart of water to boil in a saucepan. Boil the eggs in a pot for 3 minutes. Switch off the stove and allow the eggs to settle for 12 minutes. Remove the eggs from the saucepan and run under cool water. Peel them and refrigerate.

2. Pour water into a large stockpot and heat over a high temperature. Add the diced potatoes to the pot and bring to a boil. Reduce the heat and allow the contents to simmer for 10 minutes. Take out the potatoes from the stockpot and place them in ice water. Allow cooling and then refrigerate.

3. Pour the green beans into the stockpot with the water still in place. Cook for 5 to 7 minutes. Remove them and place them in ice water. Refrigerate. Whisk honey, lemon juice, mustard, olive oil, garlic, thyme, and salt and pepper in a large mixing bowl. Allow the contents to chill in the freezer for a few minutes.

4. Take out the vinaigrette from the freezer and whisk. Add the olives, capers, romaine, and tomatoes. Toss properly. Chop the boiled eggs coarsely and include them in the bowl. Slice the green beans, creating a 1-inch

length for each, and pour into the bowl containing the potatoes. Include the tuna and mix until the salad is blended. Serve.

Oven-Baked Parmesan French Fries

Wow! French fries? Are they ideal for diabetics? You may wonder. In truth, using white potatoes for this meal may not be ideal due to its high glycemic index rating. Russet potatoes are not low on the GI scale either. It contains 31 grams of starch. Hence, your consumption of this meal should be moderate. It does not hurt to throw this meal into your diet once in a while, but keep an eye on your carb intake.

Homemade French fries are healthier than those made at a fast-food chain. Enjoy your crispy potato wedges coated in flavored Parmesan cheese and other spices. It takes a total of 35 minutes to have your meal ready – 15 minutes for preparation and 20 minutes for cooking. The meal serves 6 to 8 people. Below is the nutritional information per serving for this diet.

Calories: 251 calorie

Total fat: 11 grams

Saturated fat: 3 grams

Cholesterol: 1 milligram

Sodium: 234 milligrams

Carbohydrate: 32 grams

Dietary fiber: 2 grams

Protein: 6 grams

Sugar: 1 gram

Ingredients

5 russet potatoes

¼ cup of extra-virgin olive oil

½ cup of grated Parmesan

Salt and freshly ground black pepper

Preparation

1. Preheat oven to 400 degrees Fahrenheit.

2. Peel potatoes and cut into half-inch thick (lengthwise) strips, then cut into ½-inch thick fries. Place the potatoes in a pot with 1 tablespoon of salt and cold water. Bring to a gentle boil, then reduce to low heat and cook until a paring knife tip can easily pass through. Cooked about 3/4 of the way through. Drain well and place in a mixing bowl. Add ½ teaspoon of black pepper, 1 tablespoon of salt, and olive oil into the mix. Toss properly and place in 1 layer on a non-stick baking sheet. Bake until light brown.

3. Sprinkle with Parmesan and bake for another 6 or 7 minutes, or until well-browned and crispy, and the cheese is melted and caramelized. Remove from the oven and set aside to cool for 2 minutes. Serve the food.

Pork Au Poivre

Are you thinking of a delicious French-style dish to spice up your evening? Pork Au Poivre is the right meal worth considering. Topped with a pan sauce, this food provides a lighter alternative to cream or butter-based variants. It takes 25 minutes to make from scratch to finish – 5 minutes for preparation and 20 minutes for cooking. Each serving contains 4 ounces and can serve 4 people. Here is the nutritional information per serving:

Calories: 235 calorie

Total fat: 10 grams

Saturated fat: 3 grams

Carbohydrates: 2 grams

Protein: 30 grams

Ingredients

1 ¼ pound of pork tenderloin

1 tsp of Dijon mustard

Salt

2 tsp of olive oil

½ cup of dry red wine

½ cup of chicken broth (low-sodium)

1 tbsp of black peppercorns, coarsely crushed or ground

Preparation

1. Slice the tenderloin across the length without cutting into the other end. Cut the meat into a single big, fat slice. Cover both sides of the meat with mustard and pepper. Cut the beef crosswise into 4 even sections.

2. Pour oil into a large skillet pan and heat over medium flame. Place the tenderloin into the skillet and cook

(turning once) for 10 minutes or until 155 degrees F (as registered by an instant-read thermometer).

3. Transfer the meat onto a plate and cover with foil to retain heat. Pour wine and chicken broth into the pan and cook over medium-high heat for 8 o 20 minutes, removing any bits stuck to the pan. When the sauce is reduced to about half a cup, pour it over the meat. Season the beef with salt. Serve immediately.

Ginger Tea Cake

Ginger take cake is healthy for diabetics as it contains low-calorie. It is power-packed with mouth-watering flavors from ginger, cinnamon, ground cloves, and molasses. End the day with a plate of this delicacy and wake up refreshed the next morning. Making this meal from start to finish takes 1 hour, 25 minutes. It takes 15 minutes to prepare, 15 minutes of inactivity, and 55 minutes to cook. The recipe listed below serves 18 persons. Here is the nutrition information per serving:

Calories: 139 calorie

Total fat: 3 grams

Saturated fat: 2 grams

Carbohydrates: 26 grams

Dietary fiber: 1 gram

Protein: 2 grams

Ingredients

¼ tsp of fine salt

2 cups of cake flour

1 tsp of baking soda

1 tsp of ground ginger

1 tsp of pure vanilla extract

¼ cup of reduced-fat buttermilk

2 large eggs, at room temperature

1 packed cup of light brown sugar

1 cup of canned pure pumpkin puree

¼ cup of finely chopped crystallized ginger

4 tbsp of unsalted butter, at room temperature

Kindly note that confectioners' sugar is optional.

Preparation

1. Place a rack in the lower third section of the oven. Preheat the oven to 350 degrees F.

2. Using parchment paper, line a wide (4 ½ inch by 9 ½ inches) metal loaf pan with nonstick cooking spray.

3. Get a medium-sized mixing bowl and sift the flour, baking soda, ginger, and salt in it. Pour pumpkin, vanilla, and buttermilk into another mixing bowl and whisk.

4. Beat the butter for 1 minute until smooth using an electric mixer set to medium speed. Introduce light brown sugar into the batter and beat for an additional 4 minutes until light and fluffy. Add eggs, 1 at a time, beating each one properly. Pour the flour mixture into 3 portions, proceeded by the pumpkin mixture in 2 portions, beginning and ending with the flour at low speed.

5. At medium-low speed, whisk the mixture to create a smooth batter. Switch off the mixer and add the crystallized ginger. Fold the thick batter by hand using a rubber spatula.

6. Cleanly empty the batter into a prepared pan. Ensure it has a smooth surface. Bake for 55 minutes or until a cake tester goes into the cake and comes out clean, and the top springs back when lightly pressed.

7. Allow cooling in the pan on a rack for 10 to 15 minutes before inverting the pan to drop the cake onto the cooling rack. If necessary, finish with a sprinkling of confectioner's sugar. Serve immediately.

Grilled Salad with Herbed Vinaigrette

You do not have to limit your grill surface to fish, pork, or chicken. Add vegetables into the mix. They have a straightforward preparatory and cooking process. You can ready them alongside your main meal (if any). Enjoy your low-calorie salad, topped with a savory herbed vinaigrette, before going to bed. It takes 18 minutes to make the meal – 12 minutes for preparation and 6 minutes for cooking. The recipe discussed below serves 4 persons.

Ingredients

1 tsp of Dijon mustard

2 tbsp of white wine vinegar

Freshly ground black pepper

¼ cup of parsley leaves (roughly chopped)

1 fillet anchovy, minced (optional)

3 tbsp of tarragon leaves (chopped)

4 ripe plum tomatoes, halved

1 tsp of kosher salt, plus more for seasoning

1 head romaine, quartered, root end attached

1/3 cup of extra-virgin oil, plus more for brushing

4 portobello mushrooms, stems removed and discarded

Preparation

1. Preheat an outdoor grill to medium heat.

2. If using mustard, pepper, and salt, mix the vinegar with the anchovy in a small mixing bowl. To make a smooth thick vinaigrette, introduce the oil into the mix, beginning with a few drops and gradually increasing the amount in a steady stream. Add tarragon and parsley and

whisk. Set the mixture aside.

3. Lightly spray the romaine, onions, and tomatoes with olive oil and season with salt and pepper on a sheet pan. Place the mushrooms, smooth side down, on the grill. Grill for 3 minutes, or until the juices in the cap have been collected and the mushrooms have softened. Turn them over and cook for another 3 minutes, or until the sides are mildly crispy and the core is very tender. Place the tomatoes on the grill, skin side down, and cook for 6 minutes, or until juicy and charred. Grill the romaine until the center end is soft, about 5 minutes, turning to gently char all sides.

4. Share the grilled tomatoes, mushroom caps, and wedges of romaine among 4 small plates. Serve the salads with the vinaigrette drizzled over them.

Banana Cream Pie

Cream pies are delicious – everyone loves them. However, when on a diabetic meal plan, most of them do not make the cut. A typical cream pie contains rich custard or pudding filling and comes with a whipped cream topping.

The ingredients for such a meal may include cream, milk, wheat flour, sugar, and eggs. There are many variants, including lemon, vanilla, peanut butter, chocolate, coconut, lime, and banana. However, you do not have to steer clear of this diet as we have included a diabetic-friendly recipe for banana cream pie. You can satisfy your sweet tooth with this meal in moderation. Preparing banana cream pie from start to finish takes 3 hours, 55 minutes – 35 minutes for preparation, 3 hours of inactivity, and 20 minutes of cooking. It serves 8 persons. Below is the nutritional value of this meal per serving:

Calories: 215 calorie

Total fat: 8 grams

Saturated fat: 4 grams

Carbohydrates: 32 grams

Dietary fiber: 1.5 grams

Protein: 4 grams

Ingredients

Nonstick cooking spray

2 tbsp of butter, softened

3 tbsp of boiling water

1/3 cup, and an additional ½ tsp of sugar

1 ½ tsp of unflavored gelatin

3 tbsp of all-purpose flour

2 egg yolks

1 tsp of vanilla extract

¼ cup of whipping cream

2 cups of sliced banana (3 medium bananas)

1 ½ cups of milk (1 percent low-fat)

12 graham cracker squares (6 full sheets)

Preparation

1. Preheat oven to 350 degrees Fahrenheit.

2. Apply cooking spray to a 9-inch pie plate. Put the graham crackers into a food processor and process until finely ground. Include 1 tablespoon of water and butter. Process the mixture until the crumb clumps together. Press the crumb mixture into the bottom of the pie plate and up the sides about ½ inch. Bake the contents in the oven for 10 minutes. Allow cooling.

3. Create the filling in the meantime. Pour the gelatin into a small mixing bowl. Include 3 tablespoons of boiling water; whisk until the gelatin is completely dissolved. Whisk 1/3 cup of sugar and flour in a separate medium saucepan. Lightly beat the milk and eggs together in a medium bowl. Pour the mixture into the medium saucepan containing the bowl of sugar and flour. Stir the contents for 10 minutes over medium heat until the mixture thickens and comes to a boil. Include gelatin and vanilla extract. Allow slight cooling.

4. Place the sliced bananas on the graham cracker crust. Place the pudding on top. Refrigerate the contents for 3 hours until the pudding is set.

5. Whip the cream using an electric beater. Add ½ teaspoon of sugar halfway through. Keep whipping until fully whipped. Pour the whipped cream into a plastic bag. Concentrate it in 1 corner of the bag. Cut the corner of the bag and apply slight pressure to release the cream to form a decorative pattern around the pie. Serve immediately.

Turkey Burgers with Tomato Corn Salsa

It is almost sacrilegious to toy with hamburgers because they are so fundamental to American cuisine. Substituting low-fat turkey for rich beef, as in this recipe, you risk making a drier, less-tasty burger that is unworthy of the brand. However, the vegetables compensate for the moisture factor. The burger's sauteed onion and red pepper, as well as the salsa on top, compensate for some dryness in the turkey. The Creole seasoning, in combination with the salsa, makes up for the turkey's relative lack of flavor. Turkey burgers with tomato corn salsa are low in fat, which is an ideal alternative to other burger variants. The delicious and satisfying burger takes 45 minutes to prepare from start to finish. It takes 10 minutes to prepare and 35 minutes to cook. This meal serves 4 people.

Ingredients

For the Salsa:

1 garlic clove, minced

2 tbsp of olive oil

1 tbsp of chopped fresh cilantro leaves

12 cherry tomatoes, finely chopped

1 tbsp of fresh lime juice

½ cup of cooked fresh corn or thawed frozen corn kernels

½ teaspoon of kosher salt, plus additional kosher salt and

freshly ground black pepper, for seasoning

For the Burgers:

1 tsp of kosher salt

2 tbsp of vegetable oil

1 pound of ground turkey

Freshly ground black pepper

1 small onion, finely chopped

½ small red bell pepper, finely chopped

1 tbsp of homemade or store-bought Creole spice mix

Preparation

1. To make the salsa: Drain the tomatoes in a colander for 15 minutes after tossing with salt. Toss together the tomatoes, corn, lime juice, garlic, cilantro, and olive oil in

a big mixing bowl. Toss with a pinch of salt and pepper.

2. To make the burgers: Preheat oven to 400 degrees Fahrenheit. In a small skillet, heat 1 tablespoon of the oil over medium heat. Cook, stirring occasionally, until the onion and red pepper are softened about 5 minutes. Bring to room temperature.

3. Add pepper, onion, salt, Creole spice mix, pepper, and turkey in a large mixing bowl. Season with pepper. Whisk the mixture thoroughly to form 4 large patties.

4. Get a large ovenproof skillet and heat the remaining tablespoon of oil over medium heat. Place the burgers in the skillet. Cook them until well browned, 5 minutes per side. Transfer to the oven and bake for 6 minutes or until firm to the touch. Serve with Ruthie's Summer Camp Zucchini and Oven Baked Rosemary Chips on the side.

Crispy Chicken Fingers

What sits on par with the apple pie? Chicken is the next go-to food. This delectable, cost-effective, adaptable, and simple-to-make meal can be fried, battered, or coated. For diabetics, this provides a platform for unhealthy dietary habits. You may have to watch out for sugar and carb intake. However, the recipe below provides a healthy option. It is high in protein and low in fat. It takes 25 minutes to prepare and yields 6 servings.

Ingredients

4 large eggs

¼ cup of milk

½ cup of all-purpose flour

1 pinch of cayenne pepper

2 cups of panko breadcrumbs

Vegetable oil, for shallow frying

Kosher salt and freshly ground black pepper

1 ½ pound of boneless skinless chicken breasts

Honey mustard, spicy ketchup or/and ranch dressing for serving

Preparation

Break the chicken into 3/4-inch-wide strips lengthwise. Pour the flour into a shallow dish. In a separate shallow bowl, whisk the milk, cayenne, eggs, and a pinch of salt and pepper. Put the breadcrumbs in a third shallow dish.

Place the chicken fingers in the flour. Shake off the excess and dunk into the egg mixture. Cover them in panko breadcrumbs. Set aside on a piece of wax paper or a baking sheet.

Pour ½ inch of oil in a large skillet and heat over medium-high heat. Group the chicken fingers in batches and fry for 3 minutes, until golden brown and cooked through. Place the chicken fingers on a paper towel-lined plate. Drain the contents and season with salt. Add spicy ketchup, honey mustard, and/or ranch dressing for dipping.

Seared Greens with Red Onion and Vinegar

You can enjoy your dinner over a plate of seared greens with red onion and vinegar. It takes just 16 minutes to make the meal – 10 minutes for preparation and 6 minutes for cooking. It yields 4 servings.

Ingredients

½ red onion, sliced

1 tsp of mustard seeds

Salt and pepper

¼ cup of red wine vinegar

2 tbsp of vegetable or other light oil, 2 turns of the pan

1 ½ to 2 pounds of red or yellow Swiss chard, stems removed and tops coarsely chopped.

Preparation

Heat a big skillet pan over a high flame. Add extra-virgin oil and onion. Sear mustard seeds and onion, 2 minutes. Include greens and toss with tongs in oil. Sear greens for 2 to 3 minutes. Pour vinegar into the pan. Remove the pan from the stove. Season greens with salt and pepper.

Diabetes Meal Recipes for Snacks

Meal preparation plays an essential role in controlling diabetes. Your meals boil down to specific food. But what about snacks? Are they out of the question? In truth, snacks are essential meals as the main food we eat daily, even for diabetics. They maintain blood glucose levels as close to normal as possible. With these diets, you save yourself the problem of having hypoglycemia, also known as low blood sugar. Snacking does not necessarily entail dieting on high-fat and high-sugar meals, even though most snacks fall into that category. You can create a wide range of options by carefully selecting the ingredients that you throw into the mix.

With the help of a certified and experienced dietician, you know what snacks to take at any time of the day. You also need to focus on those options that complement or improve your blood sugar levels and overall wellbeing. Know the snacks that you can consume and those to avoid.

Nonetheless, portion management is the secret to managing blood glucose (the only sugar present in the blood and the body's main source of nutrition, also known as blood sugar) and reducing weight gain. Any of the treats can be easy to digest, with carbohydrates range between 15 to 45 grams. Snacks with 15 grams f carbohydrates include:

1 cup skim milk

8 animal crackers

2 rice cakes (4-inch diameter)

15 fat-free potato or tortilla chips

½ cup of canned fruit (without the juice or syrup)

3 cups popcorn (popped by hot air or low-fat microwave)

1 cup non-fat fruit-flavored yogurt (sweetened with sugar substitute)

½ banana, 15 grapes, 1 small orange, 1 small peach, or 1 medium apple

Nuts and beans, for example, are rich in calories but low in carbs. The following are few low-carb snacks:

Cauliflower

Broccoli

Sunflower seeds

Celery sticks

Cucumber

Peanuts (not honey-coated or glazed)

If you are counting carbohydrates, do not hesitate to include them in your overall meal schedule. Stop mindless snacking while watching TV, using the phone, blogging, or walking. Be sure you have plenty of nutritious choices on hand. Check out this list of diabetic-friendly snacks organized by carbohydrate material. This section discusses diabetic-healthy snacks that you can enjoy any time of the day.

Grilled Pita Triangles

Are you looking for a wonderful party meal or something to munch while at work or on your way home? Grilled pita triangles are your go-to food. This delicacy is easy to make within 9 minutes – 1 minute for the preparation and 8 minutes for cooking. It also yields 4 servings, with 3 triangles as the serving size.

Ingredients

1 ½ tsp of olive oil

2 whole-wheat pita bread

Salt

Preparation

Get a skillet or grill pan and preheat over medium-high heat. Apply oil to both sides of the pita with a brush. Put 1 pita per time in the skillet or grill and heat for 2 minutes on each side until nicely marked. Cut each pita into 6 wedges. Sprinkle with salt to taste. Serve.

Chunky Guacamole

Is this meal ideal for diabetics? Of course, yet. Consuming avocados will not increase your blood sugar levels as they are low in carbohydrates. Even more, they are rich in fiber, giving your body the nutrient it needs. Compare to other high-fiber meals that may increase blood sugar levels, avocados are diabetic-friendly. Chunky guacamole takes 1 hour, 15 minutes to make – 15 minutes for preparation, and 1 hour of inactivity. It serves 4 persons.

Ingredients

3 limes, juiced

4 ripe avocados

Extra-virgin olive oil

1 garlic clove, minced

½ red onion, chopped

2 serrano chiles, sliced thinly

1 big handful of fresh cilantro, finely chopped

Kosher salt and freshly ground black pepper

Preparation

Cut the avocados in half and remove the pits. Using a

tablespoon, scrape the flesh into a mixing cup. With a fork, mash the avocados until they are chunky. Fold in the remaining ingredients until it is thoroughly combined. To save the guacamole from browning, place a piece of plastic wrap directly on top of it and refrigerate for 1 hour before eating.

Hot Chocolate

Are you looking for a tasty way to warm up on your way to work or at lunch, or even on a cool Saturday evening? This keto-friendly hot cocoa will satisfy your cravings. It comes fully packed with chocolate flavor, producing a rich texture that will leave you smacking your lips. The best part is that if you are on a low-carb diet, you are sure to have all of the recipes on hand.

You do not have to wait any longer for that satisfying chocolate craving as you can now enjoy creamy, rich hot chocolate with the diabetic-friendly ingredients shared below, which are readily available in the stores. It is grain-free and gluten-free. Furthermore, this recipe only takes 10 minutes to make – 5 minutes for preparation and an additional 5 minutes for cooking. The recipe below serves 3 persons.

Ingredients

1 tsp of vanilla extract

3 tbsp of unsweetened cocoa powder

2 tbsp of granulated stevia/erythritol blend (Pyure)

2 cups of unsweetened original flavor almond milk

½ cup of heavy whipping cream (coconut milk from a can for dairy-free)

Preparation

1. Combine cocoa powder with granulated stevia or erythritol blend in a medium saucepan and whisk. Break up cocoa lumps that may form.

2. Add heavy whipping cream or coconut milk, 1 tablespoon per time to form a thick liquid. Whisk the

contents.

3. When whisking, slowly pour the almond milk into the mixture. Heat the mixture over low heat, constantly whisking until it is hot. Do not allow the liquid to simmer. Remove the pan from the heat and add the vanilla extract.

4. Pour into cups, garnish if desired (ideally, whipped cream), and serve.

Salsa

Salsa is rich in nutrients and can be enjoyed with other meals, such as baked potato chips. It takes 1 hour, 15 minutes to make the meal from scratch to finish – 15 minutes for preparation, and 1 hour of inactivity. The recipe shared below serves 12 persons.

Ingredients

¼ tsp of salt

¼ tsp of sugar

½ whole lime, juiced

1 clove garlic, minced

¼ tsp of ground cumin

¼ cup of chopped onion

1 (28 oz.) can whole tomatoes with juice

½ cup of fresh cilantro leaves (or more to taste)

2 (10 oz.) cans diced tomatoes and green chiles, such as Rotel

1 whole jalapeno, quartered and sliced thin, with seeds and membrane

Preparation

1. Combine whole tomatoes, diced tomatoes, garlic,

onions, cumin, jalapeno, cilantro, sugar, lime juice, salt in a large blender or food processor, ideally, 12-cup option. If there is no large blender, blend the ingredients in batches and mix in a large casserole dish.

2. Do about 10 to 15 pulses until the right consistency is derived. Adjust the seasonings in the salsa and taste to confirm. Put the bowl of salsa in a refrigerator for at least an hour. Serve with tortilla chips.

Blueberry Cake and Banana-Nut Oatmeal Cups

These fluffy and delicious grab-and-go oatmeal cup mixes come with the sweetness of banana and blueberries. Coupled with muffins and oatmeal, you have a winner for an ideal snack. You can make a big batch over the weekend and refrigerate them for weekly consumption. Enjoy them any time of the day, whether it be breakfast, lunch, or dinner. Simply microwave for about 40 seconds before serving. It takes a total of 50 minutes to make this meal and serves 12 persons.

Ingredients

3 cups of oats

1 tsp of baking powder

1 tsp of ground cinnamon

1 tsp of vanilla extract

1/3 cup of packed brown sugar

1 ½ cups of milk (low-fat)

2 ripe bananas, mashed (¾ cup)

2 large eggs, lightly beaten

½ tsp of salt

½ cup of chopped toasted pecans

1 cup of fresh blueberries

Preparation

Preheat the oven to 375 degrees Fahrenheit. Using cooking oil, coat a muffin dish.

In a big mixing bowl, combine the oats, cream, bananas, brown sugar, eggs, baking powder, cinnamon, vanilla, and salt. Combine the blueberries and pecans in a mixing bowl. Divide the batter evenly among the muffin cups (approximately 1/3 cup each).

Bake the muffins for 25 minutes or until a toothpick inserted in the middle comes out clean. Cool for 10 minutes in the pan before turning out onto a wire rack to cool fully. Hot or at room temperature is fine.

Soy-Lime Roasted Tofu

Enjoy marinated tofu cubes with soy sauce and lime juice. Include sesame oil to give the meal the taste well deserved.

Ingredients

⅔ cup of lime juice

6 tbsp of toasted sesame oil

⅔ cup of reduced-sodium soy sauce

2 (14 oz.) packages extra-firm, water-packed tofu, drained

Preparation

To prepare the tofu, pat it dry and break it into 1/2- to 3/4-inch cubes. In a medium bowl or big sealable plastic container, combine the soy sauce, lime juice, and oil. Toss in the tofu gently to mix. Marinate for 1 hour or up to 4 hours in the refrigerator, softly stirring once or twice.

Preheat the oven to 450 degrees Fahrenheit.

Using a slotted spoon, lift the tofu from the marinade (discard marinade). Spread out on 2 big baking sheets; make sure the bits are not touching. Roast, softly turning halfway through, for about 20 minutes, or until golden brown.

Conclusion

As you approach the end of this detailed guide, bear in mind that making healthy food decisions is crucial to maintaining your diabetes and reducing the risk of complications. If you have type 1 diabetes, you should prioritize carb counting. By doing so, you can stabilize your blood glucose levels. But how do you achieve that? Calculate the number of carbohydrates in each diet and weigh it against the amount of insulin need per meal. For type 2 diabetics, especially those who battle obesity, shedding some pounds can alleviate the complications embedded in the medical condition. Losing weight can drop your blood glucose levels a considerable amount, reducing the risk of having other complications.

Some of the ways to combat obesity include dieting on low-card, Mediterranean, and low-calorie meals. Substantial weight loss will put type 2 diabetes into remission. In actuality, you either need to lose, raise, or sustain your existing weight whether you have type 1 or type 2 diabetes, so it's important to make healthy food decisions when doing so. Portion sizes come to play when treating type 1 or type 2 diabetes. With carb counting, you need to calculate nutritional facts to determine what food to eat per time. There is no one-size-fits-all portion size for everyone. What may be ideal for someone else may be out of bounds for you.

What about dieting at restaurants if you cannot make your meals? This question is essential, especially when you may not be into home-based cooking. When dining out, diabetics have a lot to think about. If you are in this category, kindly ask about the fast-food chain chef's preparation of some meat or fish. You have the option to stick to cured, grilled, baked meats, or even veggies.

Ideally, you should opt for broths instead of cream-based soups. Request that the sauce and salad dressing be served on the side. It is important to determine the meal's vegetable and carbohydrate composition. When convenient, ask for steamed vegetables. Embrace lean cuts of meat rather than those rich in fats. Trim some excess fat from the beef. Choose non-starchy beans, grilled carrots, or a sandwich instead of French fries or potatoes.

When selecting your carbs, go for whole-grain options, including pasta and wheat bread, if available. Fruits and legumes are rich in fiber and make excellent carbohydrate options for diabetics. The size of the portion is also significant. Take half of the meal home with you or split it with your table. Steer clear of these specific beverages and foods or consume them in moderation.

Sweets

Fried food

Artificial sweeteners

Alcoholic beverages

White rice and white bread

Meals with rich, creamy sauces

Nachos or baked potatoes with excessive toppings

Sweetened beverages, including soda, coffee, juice, and sweet tea

When it comes to dinner, people with diabetes have a wide variety of healthier menu choices. Controlling portion sizes and consuming the recommended levels of fiber, calcium, and healthy fats can be the key priorities. Put these factors into perspective when dieting in your favorite restaurant. Remember, alcohol is a no-no. However, some diabetics consume this drink in moderation. Find out from your dietician if you should take it or avoid it.

Being more physically involved and eating healthy go hand in hand. It will assist you in managing your diabetes while also lowering your risk of heart disease. This is how it makes the body use insulin more effectively by increasing the amount of glucose used by your muscles.

For a start, target a minimum of 150 minutes of exercise for a week. Exercising increases your heart rate. Your breathing rate increases as your body get warmer. And if you cannot go 150 minutes at once in a week, you can break down the time into smaller timeframes. For example, you may decide to exercise 5 times a week, going 30 minutes each session.

Your food journal is a good companion. You stand a better chance of losing half as much weight with this guide than if you don't have one. You will pinpoint areas of discomfort that make it impossible to treat diabetes or lose weight. It is easy to identify those areas where more carbs, fats, and calories enter your system. It also makes you more mindful of what, why, and how much you're eating.

You can avoid mindless snacking. Keep a log or use an app to keep track of your diet. Do not get frustrated if your last dietary plan flopped or you added more weight. Select the diet that matches your body's unique requirements. As such, you can escape dietary pitfalls and encounter long-term weight loss results.

Made in United States
North Haven, CT
12 March 2022